HOWL OF THE LAST FOX

The Poisoned Earth

Nara Somaratne

Publisher: Inspiring Publishers,
P.O. Box 159, Calwell, ACT Australia 2905
Email: publishaspg@gmail.com
http://www.inspiringpublishers.com

A catalogue record for this
book is available from the
NATIONAL
LIBRARY
OF AUSTRALIA
National Library of Australia

National Library of Australia The Prepublication Data Service

Author: Nara Somaratne
Title: Howl of the Last Fox
Genre: Fiction

Paperback ISBN: 978-1-923250-83-3

Meaning of Sinhala words in this book:

Aiya: elder brother

Akka: elder sister

Chena: shifting agricultural practice by clearing of forest land

Mama: mother's brother, or uncle

Mudalali: businessman

Nenda: aunt

CHAPTER 1

Death in the Village

It was January 1963, two days after the full moon. It might have been around 6 pm, not even dark, and the screaming of foxes could be heard from the paddy fields about 200 metres from our home. I was preparing kerosene lamps to light. Mother was in the kitchen preparing rice and curry for dinner. She said, 'Today, they've come early and are close to the canal.' My younger sisters Seela and Kumari rushed over to Mother, as the scary high-pitched howls continued.

Mother told us there was no need to be afraid because the foxes wouldn't come near houses and were beyond the main canal in the paddy fields.

The foxes were most active around 7 PM until midnight, according to the villagers, and then they would slowly decrease their activity the closer it got to sunrise. Fox howling was common during the rainy season.

Tonight, they had come unusually early and in a group. Around this time of year, we usually heard one or two foxes howling in the distance, their screams fading away unnoticed.

1

I normally liked the rainy season, particularly November to January, because you could hear the constant croaking of frogs and occasionally the howling of foxes during the night. This was the time of year water snakes (Sri Lankan keelback) could be found in waterways, chasing fish, lizards and other insects or hiding under leaves to catch a frog. The only problem with the rainy season was how easy it was to get a fungal infection of the foot, which caused itching between the toes. Since we never wore shoes, this was very common among the poor villagers.

My elder sister, Podi *Akka*, was in the front room with her two-year-old son Bandula. In between the ear-piercing screams of the adult foxes, juvenile foxes and puppies were also screaming, either just to follow what the adult foxes were doing or perhaps it was a habit of the group. As she served rice and curry onto our plates, Mother said, 'It must be a large group of foxes with vixens and puppies. We may not sleep well tonight.'

That would likely be the case for her and the other adults, but for us young ones, we only had to lie down on our mats, and we'd soon be fast asleep until morning.

My brother Navé was sitting on the bench in the front yard under the mango tree talking to our neighbour, Siriya. Siriya was about ten years older than Navé. Siriya had a younger sister and three younger brothers in their ancestral village in Kurunegala. They would come during the school holidays and the cultivation period. Siriya and his elder brother Samithin lived with their parents in our village.

'Senevi, go and call your brother for dinner; it is easier for me to serve all at once,' Mother said.

I went outside the house to call my brother and found everyone from the neighbourhood rushing towards Soma's house. Soma lived two houses away from our place and was the neighbour of Siriya. Siriya asked a man on the road what was happening.

'Soma has swallowed some poison,' said the man. 'We are going to find a vehicle to take her to the Yakalla hospital.'

At the village level, when someone was in trouble and needed help, it was customary that everyone came out and pitched in, forgetting their differences, at least temporarily.

Siriya and Navé went to see what had happened at Soma's house. I told the story to Mother and Podi *Akka*, who were both surprised, as Soma was such a beautiful young girl. They also came out to the front yard to see what was going on. Soma was the most beautiful girl in the village and studying to sit the Senior School Certificate (SSC) public examination at the end of the year. It seemed everyone was confused as to why Soma had taken the poison.

Loud cries—probably from her mother and elder sister— added to the ever-present screams of the foxes.

Yakalla town was about seven kilometres from our village. The main road running through the colonisation scheme connecting villages along the canal was the canal bund itself. The top of the canal bund allowed two vehicles to pass by safely. When it reached the Huruluwewa, once again the tank bund became the road. These were gravelly roads with numerous potholes, so vehicles had to manoeuvre carefully wherever the potholes were. On the high ground side of the canal were the settlements, divided into one-and-a-half acre allotments given to settlers for home gardens. The low ground side of the canal had developed into paddy fields, again divided into three-acre allotments for each householder.

The set-up of the colonisation schemes was quite different to typical rural villages. In a rural village, communities were made up of groups of houses on elevated lands surrounded by paddy fields in the lowlands. Most of the village residents were related to some extent, close or distant, as they had lived in their village for several generations.

Settlements in an irrigation scheme or colony typically were set on higher ground, with two rows of houses running parallel to the canal. In between was the access road to the houses. In our village area, on the left-hand side of the access road, allotments extended up to the canal. On the right-hand side, they were up to the ephemeral creek. Beyond the creek was the bushland, about 500 metres wide, and then a thick virgin forest. The school had been built at the centre of the village and the temple at the edge.

The bushlands were areas that had been used for *chena* cultivation – before shifting agricultural practice involving shared land for growing vegetables, cereals, and grains – but the *chenas* had been abandoned and people used them for collecting firewood and picking the plentiful seasonal wild fruits. *Eraminiya* (jackal jujube), a climbing thorny shrub with dark black fruits, *Pada wel* (bush passionfruit), and *Weera* (*Drypetes sepiaria*), with its bright red fruit, all grew by the roadside or in abandoned *chenas* behind the house. *Ma-dan* (the Java plum tree or South Indian plum tree), with its black-coloured fruit, was another. One of the most common bushes was *hinguru* (*Lantana camara*), which produced small black fruits when ripe attracting many birds. People used a tender *hinguru* stick as a toothbrush.

4

The villagers got their timber from the dense, dark virgin forest. Timber from the forest was a big help for the villagers, who used it for extensions to their houses, as well as for huts, fence posts, and making furniture.

Sometimes in the evening people could hear wild elephants trumpeting in the forest. It was common to hear the whooping of monkeys; the occasional grunts, snorts, and barks of deer; and the buzzing of insects that lived in the bark of tree trunks. Village hunters would go to both the bushland and forest to hunt game.

Next to our house, along the access road, was the carpenter George's house, and beyond our house was Siriya's. Next door to Siriya's house was where Soma lived with her family. We could hear the loud cry of Soma's mother asking for help to take her to the hospital. Soma had two elder brothers, Silva and Steven, one elder sister Chandra, and a younger brother Jaya. Silva and another young man ran to find the driver, Piyadasa *Aiya*, who had a hire car. Others went to find a tractor or even a bullock cart; they would use whichever came first to take Soma to the hospital. Piyadasa *Aiya* was a great help for villagers, since he was the only person in the area with a hire car, which was an old box-type Ford car. He was willing to be on call when people needed him, whether it was early in the morning or later at night; thus, he became a well-respected person.

It took about an hour for the car to arrive. When Navé and Siriya came back, they told us Soma had been crammed into the car with several others, and she was vomiting heavily. Her eyes were closed, and her head had fallen forward, but she was on her way to the hospital. After this incident, we had dinner and went to our mats to get some sleep, as the following day we had to go to school.

I was in year 7 and my only brother, Navé, was in year 8. Navé was two years older than me. Among eight children in the family, two of us were the only males. In the morning when we were going to school, Abé, who lived just opposite Soma's house, told us that his parents had said Soma had died on the way to the hospital. The body was being kept in the mortuary for examination. In the school, students of the senior classes and some teachers gathered round talking, most likely about the death of Soma.

when she heard about Soma's death, Podi *Akka* cried. Every time Soma had gone to the canal to bathe, she would take little Bandula with her and wash his clothes, and bathe and dry him. Even on the day she swallowed the poison, she had gone to bathe with Bandula.

The postmortem the following day revealed that Soma was four months pregnant. Her lover and classmate, Sugathé, had left the village. Sugathé was staying with a relative to go to school.

The school had a good reputation for getting excellent results from public examinations and hence attracted students from neighbouring villages. Sugathé had come from a distant place close to Anuradhapura, the capital of North Central Province. Soma's friend, the carpenter George's daughter Sumana, did not come to school for two weeks, and only after the funeral and seventh-day alms giving ceremony, a Buddhist ritual practice.

Mother and Podi *Akka* said Soma may have enjoyed taking Bandula to bathe because she was soon to become a mother herself. Poor girl, they said, she would never see her child.

No sooner had the news of Soma's death spread than the story of her pregnancy followed.

As the story went, Soma had fallen in love with Sugathé, and this had continued for over a year. As they became closer, they wanted to meet privately, but Sugathé could not visit Soma's house, as it was taboo for a schoolgirl to bring her lover home. Moreover, she had two elder brothers watching her. So, they planned to meet in the bushland behind the houses. Soma had gone to the bushland with her friend Sumana, pretending to pick wild berries, and Sugathé had come with Tikira to meet her. Tikira's family home was just behind the carpenter George's house.

This had been going on for months, with no one noticing.

Tikira and Sumana kept the secret to themselves. Eventually, Tikira and Sumana allowed them to talk privately, stepping away until Soma and Sugathé called them back. This private meeting between Soma and Sugathé developed into making love, and Soma became pregnant. When she told Sugathé the news, she had asked him to take her to his village and marry her. If he didn't, her brothers would soon find out, and she couldn't imagine what would happen then. But then Sugathé began avoiding her, and Soma mentioned this to Sumana. Eventually, Sugathé vanished from the village, and even Tikira did not know where he had gone.

On the day of the full moon, Soma went to the temple with her mother for religious ceremonies before returning home. For the next two days, she stayed at home, not communicating much with anyone. On the second day, she took Bandula to bathe as usual, then returned home to rest. In the late afternoon, she made up her mind. That evening, she went to the firewood shed and swallowed half a bottle of malathion.

After her death, Soma's devastated brother Silva rode his bicycle throughout the village in search of Sugathé, but he was nowhere to be found. Silva went to the house where he had been living but was told Sugathé had gone to his village on the day of the full moon.

That was two days ago.

At every gathering—whether at the boutique shop, cooperative store, or temple—Soma's death was the main topic of conversation. This was not the first pregnancy outside marriage—several girls had become pregnant and given birth to beautiful children.

'Soma could have done the same; she didn't need to drink poison,' said Silpa, whose daughter had given birth outside marriage. In her case, the man actually took the girl and the child to live with him, and they were living happily together.

Another villager, a man named Rala, pointed out that it was not uncommon for girls and boys, even adults, to attempt suicide for various reasons. But those attempts were by eating either *Niyangala* (glory lily), or *Weta edaru* (Barbados nut), *Olinda* (crab eyes), *Aththana* (thorn apple), *Goda kaduru* (bitter nuts), or *Kaneru* (yellow oleander) which were available near most of the gardens and in reservations. Most people who had eaten them had survived.

In the village, Soma was the first victim of the pesticide poison.

'This was the first death, but now it will become a common occurrence, drinking this pesticide poison to kill yourself,' said Silpa.

The usual blame game continued without pause. In a village, when something goes wrong, people start blaming everyone else, and so it was with this incident.

Some people said if the teachers had been more watchful and the headmaster stricter, this would never have happened. Others blamed the parents' negligence: if they had asked why the young people were going to the bushland so frequently and checked the situation out, it would not have happened. Some others thought the parents were again responsible for not having locked the poison up in a cupboard. Even the companies that brought the poison into the country for agriculture and the shops that sold it were not spared.

Gunarath *Mama* was one of the leading villagers who opposed using 'poison' in gardens and paddy fields. He was a well-respected Ayurvedic physician whom the villagers' depended on to cure most of their minor illnesses. It was only if he could not cure a patient that they would be taken to a government dispensary or hospital.

The common belief was that the companies that made these poisons were doing so not because they cared for people or wanted to improve agriculture but to maximise profits. In later years, my brother Navé and his friend Siriya had a similar view.

One day at the boutique shop Gunarath *Mama* said that our ancestors had lived in this land for more than 2600 years and never used any of these poisons on our farmlands, yet our country was called the 'granary of the east'.

'Insects are controlled by nature itself; one type of insect is another's meal, so they are naturally controlled, and we do not have to spread poison on our lands,' said Gunarath *Mama*. 'What this poison does is to kill all kinds of insects—both good and bad.'

'Soma's death was sudden,' he continued, 'because she swallowed a large quantity all at once. The rest of us absorb this poison slowly—little by little—so the death is gradual and unnoticed.'

Gunarath *Mama* was an organic farmer. He used manure and *Wetahira* (*Gliricidia sepium*) leaves as a natural fertiliser for his lands. He grew *Wetahira* along his fences, and he called the trees 'living fences'. He never sprayed insecticides or pesticides. His practice was to let the insects themselves control the insect population, as one preyed on the other. Sometimes he also used neem tree (*Kohomba*) leaves and oil to spray his crops.

Gunarath *Mama* always said, 'Look at nature, and how it controls itself. If you go against it, there will be problems. It might not be immediately visible, but it will happen.'

He continued: 'When there are lots of snails around your garden, *Ati kukula*—the greater coucal bird—will look after them, or if grasshoppers and other leaf-eating worms are around, the birds will look after them. So, the cycle goes on and we don't have to use artificial pest control methods.'

This view was respected, but many people continued to use pesticide as they believed it improved the yield.

People tend to prefer finding easy ways and short cuts.

Soma's coffin was made at George's carpentry shed, adjacent to his house. It was taken to the hospital by a tractor with a trailer, and the body was brought to Soma's home three days after her death. Tearful women cursed Sugathé and all those who supported him. As it was after school, children and schoolteachers were able to attend the funeral. The headmaster and his wife came in the morning and paid their respects to their dead student.

Many people attended the funeral as it was the first time a beautiful schoolgirl had committed suicide. Among the crowd was one special person—the newly appointed geography teacher, Mr Cyril, who was very popular among the senior students for his vast knowledge. He hailed from the down-south town of Galle in Sri Lanka, and did not know much about this new area.

One of the people who approached Mr Cyril that day was Gunarath *Mama*. After paying his respects to the schoolteacher and introducing himself, Gunarath *Mama* asked:

'Sir, the night that Soma swallowed this poison, foxes started to scream in a group very close to the canal, and we could not even sleep until midnight. Is it true that screaming foxes in a group is a signal for a bad omen? That something evil is going to happen? That's the common belief in this area. What do you think, sir?'

People gathered under the shade of a tamarind tree, eager to hear Mr Cyril's response. I was with my brother Navé and his friend, Siriya, at the forefront.

'Even Senevi can answer that,' said Mr Cyril, as everyone in the village knew of my academic skills.

'No, no, sir, I am not just asking in jest. What we have witnessed is that every time foxes start to scream in groups, something bad has happened. That's what happened during the 1957 disaster.'

Mr Cyril took the question seriously then, and calmly explained that foxes are normally solitary animals, though they do live in groups during the breeding season. If a solitary fox howls, it means he is trying to communicate with other foxes in the area.

'It is January,' he said, 'which is typically the breeding season. The mating call of a fox is like none other—an ear-piercing sound. That's why people think it is a sign of a bad omen. If you've been unable to sleep due to a high-pitched howl, it's likely a fox looking for a mate. So, once the new year comes, you'll probably be hearing foxes a lot more. Little puppies stay together until they are old enough to survive on their own, and that's when they disperse.

'Another reason is that foxes, like many other animals, are highly territorial and scream loudly to ward off rivals. However, the most common reasons foxes scream during the night is to defend their territory and to attract a vixen during the mating season.

'Therefore, there is no truth in foxes screaming being a bad omen. Foxes are an important part of the environment. They help us eradicate mice, rats, and other rodents that damage the rice harvest in your fields and clean the environment by removing dead carcasses. At this time of the year, they dig through the bunds of your rice bays to find freshwater crabs that burrow inside. It's one of their most popular foods. You don't like water leaking through crab holes in the bunds of your rice bays, do you?' asked Mr Cyril.

'Also remember, if they enter your garden, it's true they may steal your chicken, ducks, and eggs. But this is not common as foxes are very scared of your dogs and they run away and hide.

'Now tell me—what happened in 1957?' he asked Gunarath *Mama*.

CHAPTER 2

Flood in 1957

Gunarath *Mama* spat his chewing betels, cleared his throat, and began to speak.

'You see, sir, in 1957, we had lots of heavy rain. By October, the Huruluwewa tank had started to fill, and the water level was rising quickly. We cultivated our paddy fields at the right time and by December, there were rice plants growing in our fields. Relentless rain filled the tank and by the beginning of December, the tank started to spill.

'The heavy rains continued and by the middle of the month, the irrigation department announced—through a traditional messenger beating a drum (*ana bera karu*), going village to village on his bicycle—that the tank's sluice gates would be fully opened. They asked people to keep away from the canal and the overflowing tank to help protect the bund. Towards the end of the month, the rain started to cease ... but upstream catchments got even more rain, and small tanks began to overflow, meaning water came to the Huruluwewa from as far away as Sigiriya along the main natural feeder channel, Yan Oya. Huruluwewa tank was built across the Yan Oya and so large catchments drains into it.

'To explain, sir ... this is one of the largest tanks built by our great King Mahasena nearly 2000 years ago. These tanks were constructed in cascade fashion to ensure spillover from one tank flowed into the next and so on to maximise water usage. It was one of the finest irrigation systems in the ancient world, according to an irrigation engineer who spoke to us once at a meeting in the village.

'You know, sir, when it rains in December here, it really pours,' said Gunarath *Mama.*

'On the 25th of December, Christmas day, in 1957, there was a little rain in the morning, but in the afternoon, it had all cleared. Young people went to see the spilling of the tank, and we heard that the water level of the tank was rapidly rising, as more and more inflow came through Yan Oya. Some said several small tanks upstream had been breached, so it was more than direct rainwater alone.'

Gunarath *Mama* paused, remembering the events of that day.

'So, what happened next?' asked Mr Cyril.

'Well, in the evening just before dark, we heard a group of foxes screaming, and on and on it went throughout the night. I could not sleep, and Silpa from next door came over to our house. Because of the cold at night, I had lit a fire in the shed. We were drinking tea and talking about visiting our villages in Kurunegala after the rainy season. I wanted to go to our ancestral village to see my daughter, who was studying there.'

Gunarath *Mama*'s youngest daughter, Anula, was staying with her elder sister in their ancestral village and sitting for the SSC at the end of the year.

'It's the same reason I explained earlier ... it was the mating season; that's why the foxes were screaming,' said Mr Cyril.

The talk was interrupted by Podiya, a talkative lad in his teens. 'Luckily, people don't have a mating season and don't scream during the night,' he said.

'Well, sometimes women scream,' said someone behind him, and there was loud laughter.

'Shhh ...' said Gunarath *Mama*. 'This is a funeral house!'

He went back to his explanation: 'In the middle of the night, we heard a loud noise like thunder, but without a lightning strike. We heard it just once. Unable to determine what it was, we went to sleep, as the howling of the foxes also stopped.

'It was in the morning we discovered what it was—the thunderous noise was actually the sound of the dam breach. That was it. Huruluwewa dam had been breached. The misery of the people was just starting ... and that's why people in this area believe the howling of foxes brings disaster.'

By the time Gunarath *Mama* had reached this point in his story, Soma's coffin was being brought to the front yard and a monk from the village temple was preparing to deliver a sermon. The casket was closed as Soma's body was apparently swollen beyond recognition. After the religious rituals, people carried Soma's coffin to the cemetery for burial, accompanied by loud cries from some of the women. Then, people started to disperse.

One of the problems bothering me after the funeral was what had happened when the dam was breached. What was the 'disaster' Gunarath *Mama* had referred to? He had had to stop his story just at that critical point. Both my brother and I were very young at the time it happened, so we didn't know. When we got home from the funeral, we asked Mother.

'Well,' she said, 'when there was no water in the tank, there could be no farming of the paddy fields, so we only had vegetables that were grown in the garden for food. Since the dam was the only road to the outside world, villagers were trapped, and no vehicles could bring in any food or medicine. Your father had gone to our village in Kurunegala when it happened, and he could not come here for months.'

That was interesting to hear, but our curiosity remained. A few days later, after school, we went to Siriya's house to ask for more details about the disaster. Siriya's elder brother, Samithin, was home, and he told us he had gone to see the breached dam with some other youths. He had seen a massive wall of water passing into Yan Oya, overflowing into surrounding paddy fields covering several kilometres on both sides of the Yan Oya.

He said it was a terrible time to find foodstuff, so the government came to help. Initially, leaflets were dropped from a low-flying aeroplane, announcing that food would soon be airdropped. They asked the village headmen and water management officers to take charge and distribute to every householder. Without vehicle access to hospitals, several children died of curable diseases and two people succumbed to snakebites.

The screaming of foxes could be heard sometimes in the distance, but no further disasters occurred.

Aeroplanes appeared in the sky three to four times a day, dropping food packed into gunny sacks. The men ran around where the bags were dropped and collected as much as they could carry. Those responsible for distributing food only did so partially, keeping more than enough for themselves.

An incident that everyone talked about took place when an air drop occurred near the house of a villager named Badderala. His wife ran towards the gunny sack and, on her way, lost her sarong, revealing that she had no clothing underneath. She ran naked to pick up the food without even thinking of picking up her clothing. This was a topic of amusement for months and even years to come.

'It was that desperate,' said Samithin. 'The hunger caused by the food shortages overran the woman's dignity.'

'It was *not* something to be laughed at, but rather something to be ashamed of,' said Gunarath *Mama* when we asked him about it later. 'Satisfying hunger always comes first.'

As my father has gone to our ancestral village near Kurunegala, there was no adult male in our house to find food. We had to rely on the goods distributed to us, which consisted of bread, canned jam, and canned butter. Some of the gunny sacks fell into the waterways, rendering the bread inedible, so it was either discarded or fed to animals. Butter was not a familiar food item to most villagers; some people used it for cooking instead of oil. Others did not like the taste. Samithin told us that the butter was also used to lubricate the axles of bullock carts.

The water took over two months to fully recede. Boat services were established to transport people across the breach to the town of Yakalla. This was a free service, and it was very helpful to get to the hospital. Postal services also recommenced. Father came home and returned to Kurunegala frequently. Without water, the germinated paddy fields were ruined. Eventually, buffalo and cattle owners took their herds to the paddy fields for grazing.

Both yellow fever and malaria had spread in the area, and several young children died. Without mosquito nets in most houses, the only solution was to burn *Maduru Tala* (*Ocimum tenuiflorum*, an aromatic perennial plant known as holy basil), the scent of which repelled mosquitoes.

Thus, the flood caused great hardship to the poverty-stricken rural community.

By 1958, the breached dam had been repaired and was ready to store water during the north-eastern monsoon rainy season starting in October. As it was a good year for rain, people began preparing the paddy fields for cultivation during *Maha* season, which started in November.

Father was home to work in the paddy field. Being a clever farmer, he prepared the paddy field using a plough and oxen. He levelled it by using the oxen and an apparatus known as a *Poruwa* (harrow) along with some hired labour. He was very popular because he liked to recite folk songs called *Andahera Pema* (addressing the buffalo cow calls). Both my brother Navé and I prepared tea for him and the others and went to see him work. Typically, in a village, there was a tradition of mutual sharing of labour, called *Aththama* or *Kaiya*, which relied on others to help with the pressures of day-to-day work.

We collected drinking water from a clear rice bay or from the water supply field canal. One corner of our paddy field had a rocky outcrop about the size of a small rice bay. Tea and lunch were usually served on the rock, under the *Kumbuk* (Arjuna) tree. Many of the people working on neighbouring fields also came to the rock, as it was the only dry and shady spot. While drinking his tea, Father opened a small tin he carried in his home-made purse and took out a little piece of black paste. It looked just like *Goraka* (*Garcinia cambogia*) paste used in Sri Lankan cuisine. He rolled it into a small ball with his fingers and swallowed it with a sip of tea. Later in life, we came to realise it was opium, and that was why he went to Kurunegala so frequently—to buy it, as there were no opium sellers locally.

There were often some interesting talks going on while we were drinking our tea. People called our father Dasa *Aiya* (elder brother). They knew he had a good education and was knowledgeable about farming. All the settlers who arrived from Kurunegala district respected him, as he was a descendant of a once wealthy and well-regarded family, though he was poor now.

Once they asked: 'Dasa *Aiya*, what kind of paddy are you going to sow this year?' To which Father answered by giving an elaborate lecture.

'I normally like to sow in *Maha* season, when there is plenty of water available,' he said. '*Heenati* and *Pachchaperumal* are my favourite types. For *Yala* season, when water is limited, I always choose either *Murungakayan*, *Kirimurunga*, or *Suwandal*.

'You know, I don't really like growing rice during both *Maha* and *Yala* seasons. It reduces the soil fertility, which means the yield of the rice harvest reduces year after year.'

'Then what are you going to do? Just leave it?' asked Herath *Mama*.

'In our villages back in Kurunegala, we normally grow mung bean or millet, or sometimes vegetables,' explained Father.

'The mung bean and cowpea are the best, as they improve soil fertility. But here, during the *Yala* season, we often cannot plant them because excess water may kill the plants. We don't have to eat rice all the time; boiled mung beans are an equally good alternative. This year I am going to try mung bean and cowpea on bays that are not fertile and not waterlogged. Cowpea can survive severe droughts, as it needs very little water. In fact, both mung bean and cowpea need only soil moisture.

'Back in those days, when I was young in 1940 or so,' he continued, 'we tried a new variety of rice, *Pokkali,* in our Kannehepola paddy fields. That variety was good for salt-affected fields, as it is salt tolerant.'

Herath *Mama* said, 'Part of my field has salt patches; I might try to find this *Pokkali.*'

'Good luck with that,' said Father.

By this time, Gunarath *Mama* had joined us for morning tea. His paddy field was only two blocks away from ours. Managing salt was now the topic.

'If you dig some deep drainage canals with small bunds through your rice bays, you can drain out the salty water,' said Father. 'You see, salty water is heavier than freshwater, so it settles at the bottom. That's why you need to drain the channels. Remember, you must drain the salty water directly into the natural drainage channel at the boundary, not into any other bays.

'Three of my bays had salty soil,' he continued. 'I've managed to reduce the salt load, and now the rice plants are growing beautifully. Earlier, they were just bare patches. I'll show you if you follow me.'

21

After they followed Father, Navé and I had a second round of leftover milk-rice and sambal and went on our way to explore the fields and surroundings.

Under the *Kumbuk* tree, there was a little pond with reeds grown at the periphery and lots of tadpoles swimming in it. Initially, I thought they were fish, but Navé explained they were young larvae.

'During the rainy season, male frogs croak to attract the females,' he said. 'The croaking is a common sound in waterholes and paddy fields during mating season. That is why tadpoles can be seen in almost every waterhole and that is how they start their lives,' he said. He had been told this by Father.

The view across the paddy fields was breathtakingly beautiful. Some people ploughed their fields using buffaloes, as we did, while others puddled the fields—stirring up the soil and water to create a soft planting bed. With the latter, four buffaloes were tied neck to neck with ropes in a row and moved round in one spot, creating intensive tillage by hoes while the fields were under water. Then they would move to the next section in the bay. It was a slow and time-consuming process, but Father said it had other advantages, such as buffalo poo adding fertiliser to the fields.

Wherever there was any work in the rice fields, waterbirds such as heron, ibis, and egret were plentiful, gathering to eat unearthed worms, small fish, and tadpoles swept away from the rice bays. As we walked along one of the bunds, a *Kirala* (red-wattled lapwing) bird noisily circled above us, and my brother told me that when an intruder comes close to their nest, they behave this way. He said there might be a nest on the bund as usually they lay their eggs on the ground among dried sods or debris. We turned back and took a parallel bund and went to see the drainage channel at the end of our fields.

The channel collected excess drainage water from both sides of the paddy fields, and the flow passed into the Yan Oya, the main natural watercourse in the area across which the Huruluwewa had been built. From the last row of rice bays to the drainage channel, there was about two metres of reservation left on either side of the channel, and this area was kept untouched and covered with grasses, shrubs, hedges, and small trees. Some reeds were also grown along the channel.

In some fields, there were rice plants already grown, as they had been sown earlier in the season. We went up to the field of Publis *Mama,* whose sons Karu and Ari were our friends. At school, Karu was one year senior to Navé's class and Ari was my classmate. Both Karu and Ari were there, and they joined us to walk through the shrubs and reeds, but Publis *Mama* warned us to keep an eye out for snakes and foxes. He told us foxes were usually in the bush sleeping at this time of day and did not come out when people were working. But he also said a bite from a fox could kill you, as they sometimes carried rabies.

As we walked along the bunds, Karu showed us some dark-coloured poo and said it had been left by foxes the previous night. Pointing to some pieces of shells, he said the foxes might have eaten freshwater crabs. Freshwater crabs were a big problem because periodically they would dig burrows through the bunds, which made them leak.

On the other hand, freshwater crabs were useful as they fed on insects and algae from the rice bays, Karu explained. Herons and egrets would eat the freshwater crabs, and foxes too would come out from their burrows at night and eat the crabs, but only during the rice-growing season.

There were many *Kana Kokas* (pond herons) sitting quietly, as if meditating, at *Wakkada*—the small opening of the rice bay bunds where water flowed to the next lower bay. They were focused on the water, hoping to catch one of the plentiful *Puntius titteya* (small barb fish). As we arrived, they flew away to another location, showing their white feathers.

Karu was just two years older than Navé but seemed more mature as he spoke. Karu carried a long stick, and from time to time hit the ground while walking in front of us. He said the sound of that would make snakes move away as they were afraid of people. Apparently, they would attack only if you tried to kill them, so he said we should just move away if we happened to see a snake.

'Why do they move away when they hear a sound?' I asked.

Like a *pandit* (expert), Karu said, 'You know, snakes can feel the ground vibrating when we hit it, and that's why they move away.'

He explained further that snakes do not have ears like us, but they have a powerful sense of smell which helps them track and find food like rats and frogs.

Along the drainage channel at several places, people kept wooden traps to catch fish, and at the end of the day, they collected the fish and took them home.

'Those are certainly of Hawadiya *Mama*'s fish traps,' Karu said, pointing to the traps. 'He's more like a fisherman than a farmer.'

Hawadiya was Pédia's and Podiya's father, and the family lived close to Publis *Mama*'s house. His sons worked in the paddy field, but Hawadiya's interest was catching fish. During the off-season, he cycled to Huruluwewa with his fishing lines and came home with plenty of catch. On the way home, he sold some to earn additional income, and any excess fish, he smoke-dried before selling to shops.

Local people liked smoke-salted dried fish.

In some places along the field canal near drop-structures (weirs), people sometimes kept wooden traps to catch small barbs (mostly *Pethia* and *Korali*), *Kawaiya* (climbing perch), *Handaya* (panchax), *Ankutta* (freshwater catfish), and sometimes bigger *Walaya* (*Wallogo attu* or shark catfish).

There were a lot of small fish this time of the year.

When we returned to our field, it was almost lunchtime, and Mother and our elder sisters, Podi *Akka* and Punchi *Akka* had brought rice and curry for lunch. The workers washed the mud from their hands and legs using the clean water from the field canal and removed their head turban, usually a towel or a shawl used for protection from the heat. Then they would sit around and relax. The buffaloes were let loose to feed on the drainage channel reservation.

Food was served on banana leaves laid on an *Athulpotha* (small reed leave basket). After lunch was served to the workers, Mother and our sisters ate their own lunch, after which they packed the empty boxes and went to gather any available green vegetables.

Both Navé and I followed them.

First, they went to Soma's parents' field. Her father was not there, but her elder brothers, Silva and Steven, were. Soma and her mother had brought them lunch. As we approached their hut, Soma—who was around fourteen at the time—came out with a smiling face and asked whether we needed any *Kankun* (water spinach or swamp morning glory) as they had already picked some. They had a large pond in the middle of the field, and *Kankun* and *Gira pala* (*Commelina diffusa*) were common native herbs growing wild around the pond. Soma called us *Malli* (younger brother). We all picked for the day; sure, it was going to be *Mellun* (cooked salad) for dinner.

There were plenty of herbal green leaves available, again growing wild along the reservation of the drainage channel: creepers such as *Mukunuwenna* (Sessile joyweed) and climbers as *Aguna kola* (*Tylophora pauciflora*). These edible leaves provided an important part of the village diet and grew in abundance during this time.

In the late afternoon, the buffaloes were washed and released to the drainage channel reservation for grazing. All mamoties and other tools were also washed before being taken home. The buffaloes were returned to the owner, Lensuwa *Mudalali*. The following day, Father and two other people went to the paddy field with several bags of germinated paddy. These were sown manually as they walked along the muddy bays. We were given a small basket to sow by ourselves in a small bay.

That was good early training for us.

In some of the fields, people transplanted rice instead of sowing. Apparently, this gave a good harvest, as it was easy to control weeds that competed with rice plants. A month or so after sowing, Mother and our elder sisters would go to the field to remove common weeds locally known as *Batathel, Kudumetta,* and *Bajari.* This was required periodically, as the weeds kept regrowing. It was common for women and girls to pick the weeds, and sometimes children missed school to help. This was a part of village life—children had to help their parents for survival.

Teachers in the school knew the reason for the absence of students and had apparently accepted it. Rather than punishing students, some teachers held extra classes after school for those who missed their lessons.

CHAPTER 3

Challenges in the 1960s

At the end of 1959, the north-east monsoon rains arrived, but they were insufficient to fill the Huruluwewa tank for the 1960 *Maha* season paddy cultivation. Water management officers of the irrigation department visited to meet with farmers and advised that water was available only to irrigate one acre of rice per paddy field.

Father and Gunarath *Mama* asked whether they could grow mung bean or cowpea in the rest of the paddy field, which was about two acres. Some villagers opposed this, reasoning that, if everyone started doing it, more water would be needed, which would affect the rice crops.

According to Samithin, Father clearly explained that those crops required only soil moisture and did not need additional irrigation. He even explained if someone tried to divert water to the mung bean crop, the plants would die because of too much water.

'If we grow these legumes, it will be very good for the next season's rice crops and we would not need any other fertilisers,' he told them.

However, the request was declined; only a limited area was to be used for cowpea, and even that was uncertain.

After the cultivation, Father went back to our ancestral village.

Unable to make a living, some people sold their home gardens and paddy fields and left the colony and went back to their ancestral villages. Others found land in other newly established irrigation schemes such as Rajangana and settled there.

People had lost hope of making a living through farming in our village.

With the limits to the paddy fields, people turned to the forest.

Families with grown male children started to clear the forest for *chena* cultivation—one of the oldest traditional cultivation methods in Sri Lanka. This technique involved clearing patches of forest through slashing and burning to cultivate grains such as millet, mustard, sesame, and vegetables. People knew by experience, and to some degree by tradition, that the ash layer that resulted from burning provided sufficient nutrients for crops.

Alas, the destruction of the virgin forest began.

Initially, the government had banned *chena* cultivation to protect the forest and wildlife, but the people resisted the ban and threatened visiting government officials. A farmers' meeting was held in the school building and attended by government officials. They described the forest as a protected area and informed the villagers that clearing was illegal.

'Are you going to kill us by leaving us with empty stomachs?' asked one man during the meeting, who then proceeded to assault the officers. Apparently, he was drunk, according to Samithin, who was there watching.

'The forest is needed for both people and animals,' said one of the officers, who had clearly explained to the people what they were trying to do was a crime.

'You clear the forest, burn and cultivate it for one or two seasons and then abandon it,' he had said. 'For thousands of years, these forests have grown and supported wildlife. For a small benefit, you destroy it. Not just the forest, but the many wild animals who live there. They have nowhere to go. The forest is their home, village, and food source. If you don't cultivate *chena*, you can still profit from the forest. You can get all the timber you need to build your sheds, huts, and even extensions to your houses. The forest provides various types of fruits, tamarind, woodapple, and *Mora*, which are always in demand. So, if you take care of the forest, it is much more beneficial to everybody— and remember, a lot of wildlife is entirely dependent on it.'

Amid the commotion, Rala stood up and started to talk.

'You see, sir, I have five grown-up sons, and they need work. I must admit that my sons and I were the first group of people to clear the forest for *chena* cultivation. What you don't know is how much effort goes into *chena* cultivation. It's not an easy job; we cut the forest, burn it, collect all remaining timber, and make the fences to protect the plot from wild animals. We build a timber 'treehouse' in the tallest remaining tree so that wild elephants cannot reach it, and more than that, we have to stay there day and night protecting it. Throughout the night, we keep awake reciting poems and yelling out at regular intervals to scare off wild animals that might feed on our crops. I admit that we abandon the *chena* after two or three seasons, because there is no more fertile soil. We know it by experience. For the second season, we normally grow mustard, which fetches a good price.

'You can see the houses we live in, sir, and the way we eat and dress. We are poor people; we do not know any other job. We cannot cultivate our paddy fields. If we had enough money, we would not want to "fight with the forest" either.'

Only Gunarath *Mama*, Siri *Mama,* and a few others opposed the clearing of the forest, Samithin told us. Gunarath *Mama* had said it was true that the forest surrounding the villages were a great source of food, as well as providing timber. He confirmed every plant had its use as a medicine. Most people kept quiet, which was typical. In a village meeting like this, those who 'made noise' dominated and their 'voices' were counted.

But some people had shouted at the officers and apparently said to them, 'Put us all in prison; we will not stop *chena* cultivation now or in the future.'

Apparently, some people who supported the local member of parliament (MP) went to see him in Kekirawa. According to Samithin, the MP told them to continue the *chena* cultivation, saying he would speak to the Minister and other senior government officials. So it happened that the *chena* cultivation continued unabated. the forest officer in the area and other government officials were silenced, and large swathes of the forest were felled.

Even hardwood trees such as *Palu* (ironwood), *Burutha* (satinwood), *Weera* (*Drypetes sepiaria*) and *Halmilla* (Trincomalee wood) surrendered to people's axes.

31

Soon, some of the MP's supporters and relatives were involved in removing most of the valuable trees and selling them to timber mills. They even imposed a moratorium stating that forest clearance for *chena* cultivation would be temporarily halted until the valuable timber was removed. This was a lucrative business opportunity for them.

It later became clear that the MP's decision to allow *chena* cultivation in the forest was solely for this purpose, not to help the farmers.

As the forest moved away from the boundary of the villages, wandering elephants entered the *chenas* and sometimes, during the night, they entered the village gardens in search of food, damaging banana trees, jackfruit trees, and other plants as they went. One night, the trumpeting of elephants could be heard throughout the night up to several kilometres away. In the morning, the villagers found that a young she-elephant had fallen into a well when the herd had crossed the village. It took a three-day effort to rescue the elephant and wildlife officers transferred it to the Colombo zoological garden.

She was named *Hurulu Kumari* (Princess of Huruluwewa).

It was reported that in several other villages, people had shot and killed several wild elephants, while others escaped into the forest with gunshot wounds and died in abandoned *chenas*. In our village, a man was killed when an elephant attacked him while he was riding his bicycle on a road through the forest to another village.

Because of the habitat loss and fragmentation, elephants and humans began to interact more closely, creating conflict from crop raiding and injuries and deaths on both sides. Thus, the elephant–human conflict had begun.

After three months, Father came home with a lorry-load of banana, coconut, and jackfruit plants. The intention was to sell them to people and earn an additional income. He had sold or leased one of his lands in the ancestral village to find money. Being a good farmer did not mean being good at business, and most of the plants had been given to people on loan, but he was never paid for them. Father had done one good thing, though. All along the drainage channel reservation and around the rock outcrop of our paddy field, he had planted coconut and jackfruit trees. According to Samithin, some jealous farmers signed a petition and sent it to the colonisation officer, and he visited the field to inspect it. The only question he asked Father was:

'Oi, man, tell me whether you came here to eat jackfruit or rice?'

The officer then instructed all the perennial plants to be uprooted.

Father explained to him that these trees would bear fruit in eighteen months, and it was not just for him—anyone could come and pick them. Having trees near paddy fields was beneficial, as birds could nest in them and bees would be attracted to them. Fallen leaves were another good source of fertiliser, and more than that, if nothing else was available, jackfruit was a year-round food source. Back in our villages, there were gardens on all sides of the paddy fields, and what our forefathers taught us was that it helped to control insects that were damaging to rice plants and grains. Here, we only had these bushes along the drainage channel.

But the short-sighted bureaucratic officer insisted they were to be removed from the paddy field. Instead of removing the jackfruit plants, he should have encouraged others to use the reservation for growing additional perennial plants and improving their rural economy. This was the general view of the people.

After the rice harvest in March–April, the villagers were ready for traditional new year celebrations, becoming busy with buying new clothes and groceries and painting or whitewashing houses. This was when people visited relatives in their ancestral villages, young people went to town to watch movies, and in temples, people organised fundraising functions. Typically, after harvesting, common events that took place in the village were folk-song competitions and dancing, and the occasional devil-dancing to ward off evil spirits. Bicycles with ice-cream boxes and sellers of new clothes and imitation jewellery were often seen on village roads going from one village to another.

When there was money in hand, there were various ways to spend it, which was the typical pattern in village life.

The celebrations were short-lived. The dry period continued, and by the end of the year, very little monsoon rain had fallen. Hence, there was no paddy cultivation for the 1961 *Maha* season. Father went back to our village, apparently—according to Mother—to lease his house and land to his younger brother. This time, he brought a bullock cart with two bulls, only to be sold within three months. His intention was to earn a living from the cart, but he could not find work. After selling it, he went back to Kurunegala and never returned. He was bitten by a puppy, and it was only after the puppy died a month later that he discovered it had rabies.

Father was admitted to the hospital but could not be saved.

After the funeral, we returned to Huruluwewa amid the severe drought. There was no water in the canal or in any nearby small tanks. Nothing could be grown in people's home gardens because of the lack of water, so we depended on wild fruits and leaves as vegetables for our survival.

Without rice farming or *chena* cultivation, the drought brought hardship to the villagers. People cleared the forest, but there was no rain to grow dryland crops. In order to help the villagers, coupons for rice rations were distributed, with each family receiving two measures of rice (about four pounds) per family member from the cooperative shops once a week. A measure of rice cost 25 cents. In addition, each family was given labour work as a government drought-relief measure. This typically involved repairing earthen irrigation canals, filling potholes on access roads, and clearing and filling breached waterways. This was essential maintenance work for water distribution to the paddy fields when water was available for irrigation. Usually, men or youths did the work, and women were rarely seen. In our home, there were no adult males—just Navé and me, thirteen and eleven years old. At the time, our two younger sisters, Seela and Kumari, were just nine and seven years old.

Sometimes my brother and I would go out with Mother to share her work. We had two small mamoties to use. The clayey and gravelly ground was hard due to the continued drought, and when we hit the ground with the mamoties, they bounced back. Only strong men could do this kind of work, not ladies or children. But what else could we do? Mother kept working, sweating profusely, and her jacket was soaked through.

I watched her eyes filled with tears.

She was always thinking of helping the family, but she did not know which direction to take.

Most often, young people from the neighborhood came forward to help.

'*Nenda* (aunty),' they would say, 'you take a rest, and we will do your part as well.'

They often talked about Mother since she was recently widowed and did not have any grown-up sons.

As there was no green grass for the cattle and buffaloes, boys took their family's herds to dried paddy fields for grazing on remaining patches of grasses. There was still green grass along the natural drainage channel networks in the fields. I would go after school or on some weekends with my friends, Karu and Ari.

It was sad to see—the once beautiful ponds full of water lilies were now reduced to dried reeds. Freshwater turtles and mussels had died and were rotting here and there with open shells. There were no waterbirds around, such as heron, egret, or cormorant, but occasional nests of weaving birds could be found on the reeds and *Attikka* (cluster fig tree) and *Kubuk* (arjun tree) trees. Karu said some fish, such as *Lula* and *Kavaiya,* would dig deep into the mud and could survive until the next rain. They needed only soil moisture and did not need any food to survive.

'How do you know all these things?' I asked Karu.

'Hawadiaya *Mama* told us. You ask anything about fish, he will tell you. But if you ask anything about farming, he knows nothing,' said Karu, laughing.

36

During the drought, foot-and-mouth disease spread in the area, and many cattle and buffaloes died. It was a pity to see the dead carcasses rotting in the fields, some dried out with only the dried skin and bones remaining, and others with bones scattered all around where stray dogs and foxes had fed on the carcasses. Without water, the beauty and life of the landscape had gone.

Yet life would return to the paddy field with the onset of rain.

All the villagers were waiting for the rain to come; it was the only hope for life to continue.

In 1963, rain fell, but it was not enough to start paddy cultivation in *Maha* season in November. However, late season rain came in January and February, sufficient to start *Yala* season cultivation in May. With much initial difficulty, Mother was eventually successful in getting an agricultural loan for the cultivation. Then in 1964, Punchi *Akka* came home, and our economic conditions improved. By this time, Podi *Akka* had her second child, a daughter named Ranjani. After the divorce of her first husband, she remarried and went to live with her husband in Yakalla. Bandula and Ranjani grew up with us at our home.

During these difficult times, the family had now expanded.

In 1965, Gunarath *Mama*'s youngest daughter, Anula, came to school as a science teacher and took over teaching general science. She was a dedicated teacher and took extra evening classes to cover the syllabus. In 1966, I won a government scholarship to study the science stream in the city school, a central college with more facilities. Thereafter, Navé was the only male member of our family, and he stopped his schooling. I could only work in the paddy field and home garden during school holidays.

37

There was talk in the village about my scholarship win for science education at the city school. This encouraged parents and students in the village, as well as neighbouring villages, to study and win scholarships or at least pass the public examination and get jobs. Teachers were also becoming much more engaged and respected. Mr Cyril fell in love with Anula, and they got married. He had almost become a villager by this point, and people used to say how dedicated and knowledgeable these two teachers were who were now joined in matrimony. In 1970, their first child, a son, Kumara was born.

CHAPTER 4

Road to Disaster

A *nything given for nothing will have strings attached.* This is an old saying and Gunarath *Mama* frequently used it.

Rice was not only the staple food of Sri Lanka, but also an integral part of its culture and rural livelihood. Successive governments had introduced several policies and programs to increase paddy production since independence.

Once at the boutique shop, recollecting their memories of the 1960s, Gunarath *Mama* reminded his elderly friends about the introduction of chemical fertilisers.

According to the story, since 1962, fertiliser subsidies were given to farmers. The intention was initially good, to improve rice and vegetable production and hence to improve the income of farm families.

This started with commonly used fertilisers, such as ammonia and urea. People in the area believed that the most suitable fertiliser for rice paddies was ammonium sulfate. As a fraction of nitrogen was present in ammonium sulfate, rice farmers were advised to apply it to flooded soils, since nitrate-based fertilisers were a poor choice due to denitrification losses. Therefore, without any knowledge about how or when to use the fertiliser, people began using it more and more frequently because it was cheap—at the time, almost free.

Only Gunarath *Mama* refused to use any of the subsidised agrochemicals in his paddy field or in home garden. Everyone else did, though, albeit some of them at low rates, such as Siri *Mama*, Navé and Siriya, believing it would help to improve the paddy yield.

Gunarath *Mama* would say natural forest was a good example to consider. He would ask people whether anyone had seen fertiliser or pesticide being applied to the forest.

'No,' they replied.

'But the forest grows healthily, because the forest itself generates fertilisers in the form of fallen leaves, dead wood, various insects, animal poo, and dead animals,' Gunarath *Mama* would respond. 'This all contributes to re-generating the forest.' He always argued that organic compounds from the leaves, barks, seeds, and roots of trees were the best fertiliser.

He also added *Kohomba* (neem) leaves, considered to be another green fertiliser, useful for killing harmful organisms in soil and warding off other insects.

Gunarath *Mama* often emphasised that using agrochemicals and fertilisers was *not* the way to manage farms, and the total ecosystem needed to be taken into account, just like in forests.

'Nothing goes to waste; it rotates like in a circle,' said Gunarath *Mama*.

When put into scientific terms, his view was that paddy fields and home gardens needed to be managed as 'natural ecosystems, including soil microbes and earthworms'.

One could best describe this as a 'circular farming system'.

Eventually, the dirty games started.

There were stories that some farmers had taken the subsidised fertiliser and sold it on the black market at higher prices.

The provision of subsidised fertiliser to farmers continued, as it was a powerful tool for attracting rural votes during an election. Other stories that spread involved fertilisers being imported by some bureaucrats and politicians, as it provided attractive commissions for them. They quickly became rich at the cost of farmers' lives.

Thus, the original aim was lost, and cheaper, lower quality fertilisers were imported, though at a higher cost to obtain a higher commission.

The unfair distribution of fertiliser was no secret amongst the people, but no action was taken to correct the situation. People unanimously claimed that the programs to supply subsidised fertiliser to farmers were replete with fraud and corruption. There were no proper criteria for selection and the distribution to farmers was not monitored.

A widely held belief among the people was that several underhand deals had been struck between officials, and sometimes those truly deserving of fertiliser received none. They had to buy it from shops at higher prices.

There were several requests from the authorities to intervene on the issue and implement a system where all farmers who were entitled to fertiliser received it, rather than allowing corrupt officers to make a lot of money in a short time.

It was well known among the farming community that corruption at all levels was the root cause affecting the small farmers' food production capabilities. Not just the fertilisers, but all other government subsidies and aid programs also had elements of corruption that prevented them from reaching those in need—the poor and other marginalised populations.

Making your own fertiliser was the best idea to avoid dependence on others—this was the view of Gunarath *Mama*.

Mr Cyril agreed with him, saying, 'The use of organic fertilisers is the best, without question. I agree that compost and manure make wonderful soil conditioners as they encourage soil microbiology activity, which improves soil structure, but not everyone can get manure as they wish.'

He continued to say that in a natural forest environment, trees and bushes did not need fertiliser to grow because the forest ecosystem had its own natural cycle of nutrient recycling.

'Fallen leaves, branches, and other organic matter decompose on the forest floor, releasing nutrients back into the soil,' Mr Cyril said. 'This process, we now teach in science class in school, is known as "nutrient cycling", and it provides the necessary nutrients for the trees and bushes to grow. Additionally, the complex interactions between various organisms in the forest, such as fungi and bacteria, further contribute to the availability of nutrients for plant growth.

'However, in large irrigation schemes, natural forest ecosystems are not found, and the recycling of nutrients is not complete; therefore, the use of a limited amount of fertiliser is needed to supplement it.'

This was the view of both Mr Cyril and Anula.

Because of the low cost, fertiliser use—often excessive—expanded to home gardens as well. During vegetable and tobacco growing seasons, ammonia and urea were mainly used. Urea fertiliser provided the plants with nitrogen promoting green leafy growth and making the plants look lush. Since urea fertiliser could provide only nitrogen and not phosphorus or potassium, it was primarily used for foliar growth. However, due to a lack of knowledge, they tended to use it on all crops and plants.

After fertiliser subsidies were first introduced, they had been removed and re-introduced several times. The initial ammonia and urea subsidies were later extended to cover *Mada Pohora* (triple superphosphate or TSP) and potassium chloride (MOP) to increase the paddy harvest. This resulted in paddy farmers using more fertilisers than they had previously.

This was the dark side of subsidies, as no one had ever estimated the amount of fertiliser needed per crop for various soil types.

In contrast, in rice farming, some farmers spread straw all over the paddy field and burned it, believing it was a way of adding fertiliser. However, Anula said that straw ash released only a limited amount of fertiliser, mainly potassium, and therefore there would be no harm if we added a limited amount of chemical fertiliser to the field to supplement the soil nutrient, confirming Mr Cyril's thought.

Gunarath *Mama* was not convinced about using any amount of chemical fertilisers, however. He said the reduced yield was covered by the saving that came from not adding the cost of chemical fertiliser.

There had been extensive discussion on this topic at farmers' meetings attended by Mr Cyril and Anula. Like the over-used fertiliser, the use of weedicide and pesticide was another issue. Almost all the villagers at the meeting believed that insects were the leading cause of yield loss and agreed that insecticides should be applied whenever insects were seen in the rice field. However, from their local knowledge, some villagers also knew that certain insects were good for pest control and that insecticides could be harmful to these beneficial insects as well. It was not just the local knowledge, but farmers came to know this through discussion in the meetings with agricultural extension officers.

Mr Cyril asked in a meeting whether anyone could identify 'good insects' and 'bad insects', but apart from Gunarath *Mama* and a few others, most did not know, nor had they ever thought about it.

These meetings were rare; though very useful, they lacked consistency.

At the end of the meeting, Mr Cyril said that his youngest brother, Dr Piyal, would be visiting the country in a month for a holiday and that he would invite him to share insightful knowledge about agrochemical use. He was working overseas as an agricultural expert in an international organisation in South-Asian countries and had an overall knowledge about pests and pest control and types of fertilisers.

People agreed to attend the meeting.

Since Soma's death, several others in nearby villages had died after swallowing pesticides, mostly due to failed relationships or frustration over unemployment. Therefore, there was no need for any education program to convince villagers that pesticides could be harmful to human and environment health. Instructions and warnings were given on the labels, but people paid little attention. Therefore, large quantities were sprayed, sometimes at the wrong time, and most people were not even wearing protective masks.

Some people such as Gunarath *Mama* strongly believed that alternative pest control methods could be just as effective as pesticides.

Sadly, vegetable farmers across the country applied pesticides before the harvest just to make them 'look good'—that is, so the green leaves were not eaten by caterpillars or insects.

'In fact,' said Gunarath *Mama*, 'those vegetables that look good are the one that should be avoided. Better to use the ones that have been eaten by worms.'

To this, Herath *Mama* added that we couldn't even have properly ripened bananas or mangoes these days because they were all artificially ripened by spraying carbide.

'This is self-destruction,' confirmed Gunarath *Mama*. 'We have this habit of blaming governments and officials for everything, but we are not looking at what *we* are doing. For a small early profit, we feed poison to people. So, part of the blame should be aimed at the farmers as well.'

Siri *Mama* was one of the villagers who applied fertiliser and pesticides in his paddy field but not in his home garden, as he grew betel there. Betel leaves were chewed by most people and therefore, Siri *Mama* was very careful not to contaminate any of the betel with 'poisons'. He sold his betel at local shops and at a nearby town's weekly Sunday market. He was a quiet and innocent person who originally came from near our ancestral village in Kurunegala.

Siri *Mama* had an arrogant wife, Menike; villagers would say she boasted about her family and considered herself aristocratic. Some villagers had a habit of finding out about others' backgrounds. It later became known that what she said about her family was all a big lie. They had two sons, Aruna and Sirimath, a daughter, Aruni, and one adopted child, Simon, from the ancestral village.

One day, after spraying pesticides in the paddy field, Siri *Mama* passed the village boutique shop with his mask still on his face, lowered to chin level. As he stepped into the shop to buy some sugar and a tin of sardines, some people noticed that his mask was not a normal one.

The boutique shop was a popular meeting point for villagers. It served snacks such as sugar buns, hoppers, and tea, and people would visit to play games, read the newspaper, listen to the radio, or just sit and gossip. It was also common to see in all such shops at least two bunches of ripened bananas hanging on the veranda near the tearoom.

That day, Podiya and several others were playing cards at a corner table, while others were playing the board games Carrom and Daam (checkers) in another corner.

'What are you wearing, *Mama*?' Podiya asked.

Siri *Mama* told them he had bought the mask from Jamis *Mudalali*'s shop and had been told it was a 'new kind of special mask'.

'It was a bit more expensive,' he added, explaining there had been no normal masks in any of the other shops either.

'Do you know he has lied to you to sell this?' said Podiya.

'No,' Siri *Mama*'s answered.

'It is not for wearing on the face, *Mama*; it is what girls wear between their legs,' said Podiya, laughing loudly.

Everyone turned to look at Siri *Mama*, and some also started to laugh.

Confused, Siri *Mama* repeated, 'What do you mean?'

'Don't you know what the adult girls wear underneath on their monthly period days?' Podiya laughed loudly again, encouraging the others to laugh even harder, and embarrassing Siri *Mama*.

Banda shouted at Podiya and asked him to stop teasing an innocent man.

'We all know you have verbal diarrhoea, Podiya,' said Banda, 'but think about who you are speaking to. He is like your father. Siri *Mama* at least wears something. It is not his fault; it is the cunning Jamis who has sold the ladies' sanitary wear pretending it is a mask. Whatever it is, its job is done, at least preventing the poison from penetrating through the nose.

Perhaps it's better than a normal mask. Anyway, there is to be no more talk about it.'

The story did not stop there, though; it spread quickly, and the teasing and laughing continued for several weeks.

Nevertheless, whether knowingly or unknowingly, it caught on, and other people started wearing sanitary towels as face masks when spraying pesticides, since there were no other masks available in the shops.

People were that desperate.

Despite its harmful effects on human and environmental health, some people continued to believe that, without pesticides, rice could not be farmed productively, and natural control was not as effective in large-scale rice production. In time, new varieties of rice were introduced, and by 1970, almost all farmers had adopted the new varieties. This meant it was essential to use fertilisers and pest control, or so most people believed.

Moreover, there was a strong belief that pesticides improved rice yields, though this had not been confirmed.

Only a small number of people in the village, such as Gunarath *Mama*, Navé, and Siriya, never accepted this and were of the belief that pesticide use should be stopped or at least be reduced. One of their strong arguments was, what was the point of achieving a 10% higher yield if you spent a lot of money on pesticides and fertilisers? And Gunarath *Mama* always said, 'One day, if the government stops these subsidies, how are you going to afford them?'

Dr Piyal attended a farmer education program with an agricultural extension officer, arranged by Mr Cyril. Typically, a small number of people attended these extension programs, but on this occasion, there was much interest in hearing what this world expert had to say. A few farmers from neighbouring villages also attended.

Dr Piyal said repeatedly to use fertilisers and pesticides, especially malathion products, carefully, as they were highly poisonous substances. He said *Mada Pohora* (TSP) was one of the first high-analysis phosphorus fertilisers. It was a common fertiliser for promoting plant wellness and was often used for fertilising leguminous crops, such as beans or cowpea, since they did not require nitrogen fertilisers. The reduction of TSP was the main cause of yellowing in paddy cultivation. His advice was not to use excessive fertiliser that was harmful to the plant itself as well as the environment, although he did acknowledge limited use of chemical fertiliser was necessary for optimal growth and grain production in rice farming.

His advice, however, was to use organic fertilisers as much as possible. 'The continuous application of synthetic substances has adverse effects on the natural environment,' he re-emphasised.

Dr Piyal asked the farmers what they were using on their paddies, and most farmers confirmed they used TSP at 50–75 kg per acre, urea at 25 kg per acre three times (at two weeks, one month, and six weeks) in one cropping cycle, almost 150 kg. In addition, 25 kg of MOP was also added.

'This is way too high,' said Dr Piyal. 'At least 50 to 70 percent more than what is required.'

Many agreed that they were using excessive fertiliser in their fields, well above the recommended levels, as they received the products at considerably subsidised rates. At the same time, their efficiency of use was significantly low.

'What happens to the excess fertiliser?' asked someone from the back row.

Dr Piyal replied by asking a question back: 'If it was not given free or at a subsidised price, would you still apply the same amount?'

Most replied with a 'no,' but admitted they did not know how much to apply anyway.

'That is where the problem lies,' said Dr Piyal. 'What happens to the excess is that it is lost anyway and damages the soil-water environment.

'You could call it "subsidised damage",' Dr Piyal laughed.

One of the farmers asked why they must spray malathion again and again, if it was a poison.

Dr Piyal confirmed that malathion was a kind of chemical that was broken down by bacteria, which was known as 'biodegradability'.

'Sorry that I sometimes use scientific words. I will try my best to avoid them,' said Dr Piyal.

He confirmed that despite its higher environmental biodegradability in relation to some other pesticides, malathion remained a highly toxic chemical for both target and non-target insects. A consequence of its breakdown nature was the need for repeated applications.

'What this means is the development of insect pest resistance,' said Dr Piyal. 'Again, this means higher malathion concentrations are required during application, introducing greater risk to non-target plants and animals.'

Gunarath *Mama* asked about the effects on freshwater, non-target animals, and insects, and Dr Piyal confirmed they were particularly vulnerable to the impact of insecticides.

'Contamination of their home environments, such as ponds and lakes where fish, crabs, and frogs live, can easily occur due to extensive spraying—even from nearby agricultural lands,' said Dr Piyal.

Siri *Mama* asked if it affected his land, as he was not applying pesticides to his home garden.

'It will be indirectly,' Dr Piyal answered. 'This is how it happens, *Mama*. You may not use fertiliser and pesticides in your gardens, but if your neighbours use them, the excess chemicals can carry via surface water to your land and deposit when it rains. This will finally end up in waterways such as canals, lakes, and reservoirs.

'And that is not the end,' he continued. 'When the rainwater moves through soil, it dissolves some excess chemicals and carries into groundwater. Groundwater does not stay in one place; it moves slowly down gradient and may come to your well and contaminate the well water, even though you did not use any fertiliser or pesticides in your garden. This process is very slow, and it takes years for its effects to be noticeable. In most cases, when we notice, the damage has been done.'

'It may already be happening,' said Siri *Mama*.

'It could very well be,' said Dr Piyal. 'That is why we must limit the use of fertilisers and pesticides to protect the environment and all that depends on it—and that includes us humans. Dr Piyal further elaborated that once the poison moves to groundwater, there is no way to control its movement, affecting everyone who drinks the well water. He also reminded that while heavy metals like arsenic and cadmium move through soil to groundwater slowly, they can take several years to damage the human body, particularly the kidneys.

'The damage is not just to humans; it wipes out all kinds of insects, including butterflies, dragonflies, bees, and even earthworms,' he said.

Gunarath *Mama* said, 'Imagine the world without bees and earthworms. They are the two pillars of agriculture, certainly not the fertiliser nor the pesticides. This is what we learned from our ancestors.'

Dr Piyal added that earthworms had existed for over 500 million years and they could live up to eight years, playing a crucial role in creating nutrient-rich soil.

'And that service we are going to destroy by continuing to spray pesticide,' said Gunarath *Mama*.

Dr Piyal said that other pests, such as grasshoppers, beetles, and leafhoppers, could attack and damage the leaves of the plant, making it difficult for the rice to ever reach grain production. In addition to these, grain-sucking insects like stink bugs feed on the rice grain itself, permanently stunting its growth and reducing yield.

Dr Piyal picked up a book he had brought with him and opened it to show pictures of various beneficial and harmful insects. He had even brought colour-printed pages of the book, which he distributed to each participant.

'Look for these four beneficial insects,' he said. 'Spider (*Araneae*), lady beetle (*Micraspis discolor*), damselfly (*Coenagrionidae*: Odonata), and Asian honeybee (*Apis cerana*). These are your friends, not pests.'

Again, displaying pictures, he asked the audience to identify insects that were serious rice pests, but very few could name them. He said, 'Don't worry about the proper name; what do you normally call them? *Panuwa* (worm)—I am sure you all know that one, and another very common pest in the paddy field is *Keedawa* (brown plant hopper). My intention is not to give you their proper name. You're not school students, you don't have to remember their names. Just know the damage they can do, and how to identify them in your fields.

'*Keedawa* causes yellowing and drying of plants. Another common pest is the rice leaf folder (*Cnaphalocrocis medinalis*), whose larvae scrape away the green tissues from the leaves. There's the Asian rice bug (*Leptocorisa sp.*), whose larvae, upon hatching, bore into the stem and begin feeding. Leaf miner *(Hydrellia sp.)* adults lay their eggs on the leaf's surface and then its larvae burrow into the leaf. The rice caseworm *(Parapoynx stagnalis)* is a species of moth whose larvae feed on the leaves. Then there's the yellow stem borer (*Scirpophaga incertulas*), found in aquatic environments where there is continuous flooding; second instar larvae enclose themselves in body leaf wrappings to make tubes and detach themselves from the leaf and fall on to the water surface. The striped stem borer (*Chilo suppressalis*) is another kind of moth and larvae that bore into the stem. And the Asian rice gall midge (*Orseolia oryzae*) is a small fly like a mosquito that causes damage, including the formation of a hollow cavity or tubular gall at the base of the infested tiller.

'These are your enemies,' said Dr Piyal. 'They should be the target to eliminate.'

He went on to further emphasise that these pests would not all be present at the same time—that maybe only one or two would be seen in the one season.

'You apply pesticides in limited amounts only *when you see any of these pests, rather than as a precaution*. Otherwise, it will kill all good and bad insects and particularly wipe out crabs and fish from your paddy fields.

As Dr Piyal paused to take a breath, people started to ask further questions.

'How does that happen? You mean it affects even crabs?' Herath *Mama* asked.

'Just like when we grow up, we outgrow our clothing; crabs do the same,' said Dr Piyal. 'When they outgrow their shell, they shed it and a new one starts to grow. Pesticides can interfere with various aspects of growth and the normal moult cycle of a crab species. Both crabs and fish spend most of their life cycle in, and proximal to, sediments of the rice bays in which pesticide residues can reside. This will affect the fish and crab population in rice fields and other waterways.

'And it does not stop there. When dead fish and crabs are eaten by frogs, birds, and foxes, they also absorb the poison into their systems, potentially wiping out entire ecosystems!

'Now you see the damage,' he continued. 'We must not look at our gardens and paddy fields simply as sources of food for our survival. They have colonies of insects that depend on them. It is like a chain: we must not allow a link to be broken. If we do, ultimately, we are the losers. And anyway, if there are birds present, nesting close by, they will eat most of your "bad insects".'

Dr Piyal continued to further elaborate, explaining that the environment is made of interconnected and overlapping links in the food chain. Once it is broken, there would be no such things as frogs, crabs, spiders, and birds to eat the 'bad' insects. It is like an interconnected web, all linked to each other.

'Sadly, without knowing this, we produce food today that threatens both people and nature, degrading our land and water,' he continued. 'Pesticides can contaminate soil, water, and other vegetation. In addition to killing insects or weeds, pesticides can be toxic to a host of other living things, including birds, fish, beneficial insects, and non-target plants. Their residues can remain in water and other components of the environment.'

'That is why we don't see any earthworms when we dig the soil,' said Herath *Mama*.

'Did you know just one bird can eat more than 300 caterpillars *or* at least 100 grasshoppers every day?' said Dr Piyal. 'They need more food during nesting season: one nest with at least three chicks may need around 6000 caterpillars. Chicks need more food as they grow fast, as they're always hungry.

'This is one of the best "pest control methods" nature has given us, but sadly we are not using them.

'It's amazing—his is what Navé's father Dasa *Aiya* always used to say,' said Gunarath *Mama*.

Dr Piyal talked about some of his experiences in other countries. He said it was normal that land was subjected to degradation due to improper agricultural practices and excessive use of chemical fertiliser. Therefore, modern cultivation methods had developed and were being actively adopted to get high yields from available land.

'That is what everyone wanted, isn't it?' he asked.

Dr Piyal continued, saying that humans had produced these chemical fertilisers, which provided the plant with artificial nutrients such as nitrogen, phosphorus, and potassium found in the natural soil necessary for plant growth.

'But any excessive use of chemical fertilisers on agricultural lands will not give you more yield,' he said. 'Some people think adding more fertiliser means they will get more and more yield, but that is not the case. It just causes great damage to the natural environment and animals—and that includes us humans, as I have said already.'

'Then how do we determine the right amount to use?' Herath *Mama* asked.

'The best way is to test the soil,' Dr Piyal responded. 'You should only supplement already available composting activities. Remember the tiny little things living in the soil that are so important—what we normally call "soil microbes" or "bacteria"? They are plentiful in natural soil and in compost fertilisers, not what you "buy" from subsidised schemes.

'Unless they give "subsidised bacteria"!' Aruna laughed from a seat at the back.

There were several other comments targeting politicians and senior government officials, but Dr Piyal ignored them and continued.

'In the early days, farmers used more natural fertilisers and fewer synthetic ones. But nowadays, chemical fertilisers are subsidised, and people have become lazy when it comes to making their own natural fertilisers. Almost all useful soil microbes, including earthworms, have been wiped out due to excessive pesticide and fertiliser use.

'I've never heard any of this before,' said Herath *Mama,* who was sitting next to Siri *Mama.*

'These are the things the government should have been telling you, instead of just providing subsidies,' said Dr Piyal.

'There is no doubt that chemical fertilisers increase crop yield, but their overuse hardens the soil, decreases soil fertility, and increases toxic heavy metals into the soil and water, creating hazards for humans, insects, other animals, and the environment.

'The increase in crop yield is needed to reflect all the additional costs: the cost of adding fertilisers and pesticides; the cost of damage to the environment, insects, and other animals; and the cost of damage to human health.

'Is it worth it?' asked Dr Piyal. 'I think not. The overall overuse of fertilisers has no positive outcome.'

People admitted that what they were actually doing was poisoning the environment and slowly destroying it. The farmers who attended were most appreciative of this new information Dr Piyal had given them and thanked him profusely for his time in the village.

CHAPTER 5

The Second Generation

The 1970s brought employment problems and a demand for additional land for cultivation, but there was no more forest left to clear. The second generation was the hardest hit among the colonists, and they, along with the third generation of settlers, started building settlements in abandoned *chenas*. Ironically, these included the descendants of the very people who had once fought for *chena* cultivation. The tracts were developed into access roads.

The real issue, however, was people's mindset. They firmly believed that paddy cultivation was essential for survival, and they saw no alternative during the off-season or drought years.

'What a surprise!' Gunarath *Mama* exclaimed.

'The same areas their fathers abandoned because "the soil is not fertile after two cultivation seasons" have now become their children's farmlands and settlements,' said Gunarath *Mama*. 'Had they spared the forest, we would at least have something left to cultivate, as well as our home gardens.'

Siri *Mama* responded, 'They didn't want to cultivate home gardens—they just wanted freshly burned forest.'

'Nothing comes easily,' said Gunarath *Mama*. 'One must work hard to get what one needs. But people are always looking for easy ways and shortcuts.'

The economic condition of the villagers did not improve because of *chena* cultivation. Only those who successfully completed public examinations at school and went on to university managed to find employment with the government or in the public sector. Some lucky ones secured teaching or clerical jobs after the SSC, others joined the police force and the military, and a few found overseas employment in the Middle East as domestic helpers, mechanics, and tradesmen. Their 'family economy' improved, but certainly not because of farming.

Most of the young people were unemployed, waiting for the next season to cultivate.

In 1971, frustrated youth took up arms against the government, demanding change in an underground political movement that spread throughout the country. However, they were later brutally defeated by the government.

In 1972, I came home after my advanced- level examination. Rather than staying at home waiting for results, Siriya and I started growing vegetables in the paddy field. It was May. We decided to grow up-country vegetables, which had a good market, and vowed never to use agrochemicals or fertilisers.

Siriya had more background knowledge about the impacts of agrochemicals on human health and the environment, as well as firsthand experience listening to Mr Cyril, Dr Piyal, and agricultural extension officers, and Gunarath *Mama* on natural insect control.

We chose an area close to the drainage channels on Siriya's paddy field and dug a well for watering in the dry drainage channel bed. We fenced the area, built a hut, and collected manure as we walked through the paddy fields.

One day at the boutique shop, people were discussing our plan when Siriya entered.

'We heard that you and Senevi are going to start growing up-country vegetables here—do you think it will work? It's never been done before,' one man said.

'We must try first and see the results later,' was Siriya's short reply.

'Those kinds of vegetables need a cool climate—that's why they grow them in the up-country,' said another.

'This time of year, it's like a desert here—no rain and dry all the time,' someone else added. 'If it works, it is a miracle … but if you succeed, it'll be a good lesson for us all.'

Siriya appreciated this little bit of encouragement and positive thinking.

We walked through fields in a grid pattern, carrying gunny bags to collect cow manure. There were plenty of buffaloes and cows wandering around, feeding on whatever remained near the drainage channels, as well as dry grasses and rice stalks.

Within a week, we had collected a pile of manure that was more than enough.

By this time, our seeds had germinated. After preparing the vegetable beds, we planted beetroots, cabbages, leaks, carrots, parsnips, and turnips. With regular watering and manuring, a lush vegetable garden soon emerged in the middle of the golden rice straws in the dry paddy field.

To protect the plot from vandals and wandering animals, we stayed in the field day and night. During the daytime, we worked in the vegetable plots, and at night, we sat outside the hut, gazing at the star-filled sky, talking, or reading.

The dark blue sky was empty of clouds. Except for the occasional sound of crows in the evening, the nights were quiet. Before dark, one of us would take turns going to the village to bring back dinner. Some nights, only one of us stayed in the paddy field to watch over the vegetable garden.

One day, Siriya said he had seen a fox wandering around the plot in the evening. Normally, at this time of the year, after the harvest, foxes would come out from their dens or hiding places in search of food—rats feeding on fallen rice grains and rabbits.

Two weeks after that first sighting, we were both staying at the plot overnight, as the vegetables had grown quickly, and we were planning to start harvesting within a month. It was the night of the full moon in August when we heard a fox howling from our paddy field. The sound came from the direction of the rock where we usually had our lunches.

Sure enough, there it was—a single fox sitting on top of the rock, howling. We could see it clearly in the twilight of the evening. The following day, we put some leftover food outside the fence to see if the fox would come back in search of food, but it never returned.

After that, we never heard the howling of foxes in the area, even during their mating season. Nor did anyone else.

Never again.

By this time, I had become close friends with Mr Cyril and Anula, and we often visited each other. One day, Mr Cyril said that the use and overuse of malathion had disrupted the food chain of animals, even large ones like foxes. Foxes were the last predator in the food chain, and when primary consumers like grasshoppers, rats, crabs, and frogs were wiped out, the predator could not survive.

He repeated that the excessive use of pesticides was the primary cause.

Not only that, but it also damaged soil microbes and earthworms, slowly destroying the environment. He said the natural environment was changing so fast that there were no more fish and frogs in the paddy fields, and no earthworms in the gardens. Everything was starting to disappear.

To the delight of Gunarath *Mama*, Mr Cyril said that schools had introduced the teaching of biodiversity and the importance of protecting it as part of environmental science classes.

In August, I received a science teaching appointment at a school about eight kilometres away, and Navé took over the work at the plot. The vegetable farm was successful, and many people realised there were other ways to earn money rather than waiting for rain or relying on paddy or *chena* cultivation. The most important part was that it had been grown entirely without pesticides—only manure was used to fertilise the soil.

For the first harvest, Siriya and Navé invited Gunarath *Mama* and a few others to visit the plot. It became a talking point in the village—people began to see that they could earn money by cultivating vegetables, mung bean, and cowpeas rather than depending solely on rice farming. And this time, the talk was all positive about growing vegetables as an off-season cropping option.

People from distant villages came on their bicycles to buy vegetables and sell them at their village markets. The produce was cheaper than the up-country vegetables brought in by lorries, and it was freshly harvested. This created secondary employment opportunities and allowed people to enjoy fresh, pesticide-free vegetables.

Most people realised this was a far better option than *chena* cultivation.

The second and third generations of the original settlers had begun building their homes in abandoned *chena* land. These areas were cleared, fenced off, and buildings were erected. Home gardens were established using water from dug wells, but they still largely depended on rainwater. Only perennial plants such as coconuts, jackfruits, and bananas were watered using well water during dry periods. During the rainy season, people grew chillies as a cash crop, along with vegetables such as eggplant and pumpkin.

However, people began overusing fertilisers even in their home gardens, mostly due to a lack of knowledge about how much to use and when. Some years, people attempted large-scale farming, sometimes borrowing money to support their efforts.

One of the first 'second generation' settlers to move into the abandoned *chena* was Podiya's elder brother, Pédia.

He fenced off about three acres of land and started cultivating it. He had five daughters to feed, so he and his wife had to work hard. In addition, he took on daily labour jobs to earn extra money.

'Life here is a struggle—a never-ending struggle,' Pédia would often say.

Watering the gardens was one of the hardest tasks. A large-diameter well had been dug with government funding, but people had to borrow money to buy water pumps.

A meeting was organised, and land officers and irrigation officers came to advise on the limitations of groundwater use. They explained that the underground water table was over fifteen metres deep, and in some areas, even deeper. The water-bearing rock was weathered bedrock, and in some cases, it was fractured, meaning it had a low yield. Large water pumps could not be used to extract large quantities of water.

Because groundwater replenishment was slow, careful usage was necessary, the officers said.

'Why do you say, "slow replenishment", and what is "replenishment" anyway?' asked Pédia.

This time, the officer used simple words to explain.

'You see, here we do not irrigate, nor do we have canals running through this area. Water reaches the land only when it rains, and that happens for just a few months during the two rainy seasons. When it rains, only a small portion of the water penetrates the soil and moves slowly downward to the underground water reservoir, becoming groundwater. Some scientists estimate that this is less than 10% of the total rainfall, so the amount is very small,' said the officer.

Pédia had never owned a paddy field of his own. His father's land and paddy field were given to his brother Podiya. However, every year he cultivated 4-5 acres of rice as an *Anda Goviya* (tenant farmer), ensuring he never faced a shortage of rice for his own consumption. The surplus was sold, providing him with a consistent income. He also built a large house on their land.

Since its introduction, the fertiliser subsidy had become a customary practice, and successive governments were under immense pressure to continue it despite budgetary constraints. The subsidy policy evolved over time and was provided for all three main types of fertilisers: nitrogen (N), phosphorus (P), and potassium (K)—primarily targeting rice crops.

Paddy farmers were eligible to apply for the fertiliser subsidy if they had legal title to their paddy fields. However, once purchased, fertiliser was often applied to paddies cultivated on lands without legal titles, as well as to crops other than rice. This was a common problem.

In theory, tenant farmers without land ownership were also entitled to the subsidy, but they needed to provide documentary evidence of their cultivation rights. Pédia said he never received subsidised fertiliser because the landowner claimed it instead. In most cases, tenant farmers had to purchase fertiliser at a higher price.

For vegetable cultivation, whether it was during the off-season in paddy fields or *chena,* the results were the same. There was renewed interest in growing vegetables for markets spread across villages, with chilli, eggplants, and pumpkins being grown in abundance. Some people invested all their savings and even pawned family jewellery to fund their farms.

Maintaining the gardens was not easy—daily watering and periodic application of fertilisers often required hired labour. Large-scale growers expected big profits.

Navé owned a one-acre plot bought from a farmer, which had previously been abandoned *chena*. He hired labourers to dig a well and planted chillies.

In addition to financial struggles, farmers faced droughts and floods, both of which could devastate crops and reduce yields, impacting their livelihoods. Another major challenge was marketing their harvest. Farmers often had to transport their produce to local markets on foot or by bicycle, a time-consuming and exhausting task. As a result, they were often forced to sell their produce at extremely low prices because they could not afford to transport it to areas with higher demand.

Middlemen, known as vegetable collectors, purchased produce from small farmers and transported it to city markets, selling it at significantly higher prices. Some farmers attempted to circumvent middlemen by pooling resources to hire a tractor with a trailer or even a lorry to transport their goods to newly established marketing centres. However, the prices offered were usually so low that they barely covered the cost of transportation.

There was no alternative—once the produce had been harvested, it couldn't be taken back home. And even if they did, what else could they do with it?

Farming life was full of frustrations, and, according to newspaper reports, some farmers had even taken their own lives when they couldn't repay their loans.

Dried chillies were in demand year-round, as chilli was an essential ingredient in Sri Lankan cuisine. Farmers harvested ripe chillies and sun-dried them to produce red-hot dried chillies. However, when it came time to sell, prices dropped due to an influx of imported dried chillies.

This was a deliberate tactic used by businessmen who imported agricultural products with the backing of senior government officials and politicians. There were no import restrictions to protect the local farming community. During the off-season, importation was reduced, and the cheap local dried chillies—previously bought at rock-bottom prices—were resold at inflated rates.

They were gambling with farmers' lives and the country's future. This was the common belief throughout the farming community.

People had no support—just an endless struggle to sell their produce at the lowest possible price.

One day, Navé and some other farmers took their eggplants and green chillies to the market. The prices were so low that they ended up having to cover the cost of the hired tractor and trailer from their own pockets. There wasn't even enough money left to pay for transport.

That evening, Navé stopped by the boutique shop and listened to the opinions of the locals.

'We heard you got a good price for your eggplant and green chillies?' Podiya said, tongue-in-cheek.

'Yeah, that's what we get for all our sweat,' Navé said. 'There is no market for us. Sometimes, I wonder what the point of farming is when the market is flooded with imported chilli. When we grow onions, it's the same story. I heard up-country potato farmers are struggling too.'

Poor farmers were getting hammered from all sides: flood, droughts, loans, pests, government officials and politicians, greedy businessmen … the list went on.

Podiya agreed and apologised to Navé for his cheeky comment. 'You're right about the politicians and bureaucrats,' he said. 'They're the biggest pests, but no pesticides will work on them!'

Podiya laughed loudly at his own joke, and then said, 'These people come around here with a big smile, and distribute ten kilograms of rice-to-rice *farmers*, kiss babies, and we fools keep voting for them again. Then, we don't see them for the next five years—until the next election.'

'It's part of the culture now,' said Navé, 'Vote … blame and vote again … blame … and … vote … again.'

'That's what happens when everyone grows the same thing at the same time,' said Siri *Mama*. 'We must think of diversifying what we grow.'

Herath *Mama* nodded in agreement.

'Well, it's okay if one or two farmers like both of you diversify what we grow,' said Navé, firmly yet respectfully. 'But what happens if everyone starts? And how many crops are there to diversify? The underlying problem is lack of transport. It's beyond our control.

'What the government has done is to supply imported agrochemicals at low cost, but they haven't given any help in how to sell the produce,' he continued. 'This is simply because, if we produce locally, they miss the import commission. So, their interest is always in large-scale imports. They love it—importing anything. Remember, they once imported *Kankun*.'

It was the view of many that the government couldn't profit from small producers like them. Hungry for the commission on imports, those who were supposed to look after the farming community turned a blind eye to their very real problems.

In 1977, the remaining forest in the area was declared the Huruluwewa Forest Reserve, a national park connecting two already existing national parks—Ritigala and Minneriya. By this time, about six kilometres of virgin forest had been cleared for *chena* cultivation. The forest reserve became popular among locals and tourists who visited to see wild elephants, leopards, rusty-spotted cats, and star tortoises.

Since *chena* cultivation had ceased and all the abandoned chenas were now occupied by second-generation settlers, once freely available vegetables like Thai cherry eggplants were no longer found. Some people began growing these once-wild vegetables in their home gardens as crops. With fertilisers available at low cost, people used them to increase yields for sale. One of the most popular crops was maize, as dried corn fetched a good price as poultry feed.

When one person started something, everyone else wanted to do the same. That was the common practice in the villages.

During years when water was scarce for paddy cultivation, farmers were allowed to grow soybeans in the paddy fields during the *Yala* season. However, this was short-lived, as soybean prices plummeted at harvest time. Unable to process the beans for domestic consumption as easily as rice, farmers sold their harvest at any price.

The same old drama.

Finally, they abandoned it.

After a brief period of teaching, I entered university to pursue a civil engineering degree, graduating in 1978. This marked a turning point in village life.

When Kumara finished his primary education, Mr Cyril's family moved to Galle to provide their children with a better education, but they visited and stayed with Gunarath *Mama* during most school holidays.

Navé married a girl from nearby Nikawewa village and lived in the same house in the village. I bought a house close to Kurunegala and our family moved to live there in 1980. My life took a dramatic turn after my marriage in 1983 and we moved to Australia in 1986. After further studies, I found good employment in Oman and every year we visited Sri Lanka until 2012. After that, there was a long period of absence before my return in 2019.

Throughout these years, Navé and his family continued working and living in Huruluwewa. They faced many difficulties—droughts and floods affected agricultural sales, and there was an increasing problem of wild elephants raiding crops. The elephants came from the national park in search of food.

Navé's niece, Ranjani, lived close to the national park in Nelun Wewa, a second-generation colony at the edge of the forest reserve.

Ranjani and her husband, Weeré, developed four acres of land, planting coconut, jackfruit, lemon, and banana trees. They dug a large-diameter well to irrigate the land, but it was hard work since they had no water pump.

Their house was small, and they had three school-age children. One day, Ranjani asked Weeré if it would be a good idea for her to work in the Middle East as a domestic worker for two years.

'It is a good idea—can you do that?' he answered.

Ranjani said there were many ladies going to the Middle East for work, and with their salary they could build their houses, but that she would be worried about the children and their schooling without her.

'Don't worry about them,' said Weeré. 'I will take care of them. I will never leave them alone in the house.'

So, Ranjani went to the Middle East on a two-year contract. Each month, she sent part of her salary home. When they had saved enough money, Ranjani asked Weeré to buy a water pump and start building their new home.

Ranjani was lucky in two ways. Firstly, she had a good family to stay with in the Middle East and they never mistreated her.

Secondly, Weeré saved the money Ranjani sent home. Weeré did not drink or smoke, and he spent all the money Ranjani sent wisely.

Unfortunately, this was not the case for everyone. Some irresponsible men wasted their wives' hard-earned money on alcohol, entertainment, and even affairs.

Thus, a new kind of social problem emerged.

When Ranjani returned, she was overjoyed to see the house partially built, the well-constructed with a stone wall, and a pump house with a functioning water pump. The perennial trees had grown rapidly with well water and fertiliser.

'Soon, we will be self-sufficient,' said Weeré.

However, protecting the gardens was difficult, as wild elephant raids became more frequent.

One time, when elephants destroyed their banana and coconut trees, Ranjani cried.

'It's my hard-earned money,' she sobbed. 'And it's become an easy food source for the elephants!'

On one occasion, a man was attacked by an elephant, breaking his back and leaving him bedridden. In another incident, villagers shot and killed an elephant at the forest reserve boundary.

It was a she-elephant with a calf.

All night, the elephants trumpeted in mourning, and by morning, the herd had moved deeper into the forest. Only the calf remained, desperately trying to raise its fallen mother, unaware that she was dead.

This continued for an entire day.

The herd lingered nearby, breaking branches as they moved.

'They'll never leave the calf,' one man said.

'Elephants have better qualities than some people; they never abandon their fallen,' said another man.

Some people cried seeing the calf caressing its dead mother and trying to raise her.

'Wake up, wake up, Mother, from your sleep—I am hungry now,' the calf must have been thinking.

Government officials arrived with the police to investigate the killing of the elephant. A public outcry followed, with people demanding an electric fence to protect their gardens and human lives. People of all ages gathered to see the 'dead giant', some complaining about raiding elephants destroying crops and even damaging their houses.

The officer calmly said, 'Elephants are not raiding your garden.'

A villager reacted angrily, 'Can't you see here what they have done? Look at the damage to our houses and gardens.'

Several others expressed their agreement with the angry man.

What they all asked for was compensation for the damage to their houses and crops. However, the officers reiterated that the purpose of their visit was not to assess property and crop damage but to investigate how the wild elephant had been killed and to gather evidence on who was responsible.

More people became angry, and one of them asked the officers why the elephant was considered more important than human lives.

The officers said firmly and quietly, 'They are a protected species.'

'Are we not protected?' the people began yelling over and over. 'Look at how much damage has been done to us!'

'This was their feeding ground before you came here,' said the forest officer. 'It was once *their* land, and *you* have raided it. Can't you understand that simple truth? An elephant needs at least 150 kilograms of leaves to feed on daily, so just imagine a herd of twenty elephants and how much they eat. That is why most of the day, they spend on feeding. They need a large block of forests, not small pockets of forest reserves here and there for foraging. They have nowhere to go, except this forest. This is where generations of elephants have lived.'

One of villagers replied, 'You see, sir, we are battered by every side: the rain, the drought, a minimal price for our produce, and now by wild elephants. Tell us, what should we do?'

The officer opened a folder and pulled out a letter written thirty years ago by the then-forest officer. He read it aloud and then said, 'You see, your fathers asked to clear the forest for *chena* cultivation, and at the time, the forest officer clearly explained the consequences.'

'We understand the past mistake,' said the villager. 'But now, at the very least, we need a permanent electric fence.'

A member of the village council, who was also the local MP's supporter, stepped forward and said that the MP had promised them, within a year, it would be done.

The villagers became even angrier at this, while the government officials remained silent.

'Their aim is to get the contract to earn from it—not to protect us,' said one of them. 'We know a man can pull an electric fence out, let alone an elephant.'

It was this MP's father who had been allowed to clear the forest for *chena* cultivation thirty years earlier, simply because he wanted to extract and sell the valuable timber from the forest.

'Like father, like son,' said a villager. 'Whatever way they can find money, they'll do it.'

The MP's supporter, the village councillor, tried to intervene, but people prevented him from getting further involved and chased him away.

An old, bearded man made his way to the front of the crowd with the help of a walking stick. His sunburned, wrinkled upper body was partially covered with a shawl.

'Sir, my name is Rala,' he said. 'I was one of those who started *chena* cultivation. I was in that meeting at the time, and more than anyone else here, I know what destruction has been done. Back then, we had no other option. It's true that elephants are entering farmlands, eating crops, and trampling fields in a single night. A farmer's entire annual income can be lost overnight.

'One of the damaged houses belongs to my third son. He died of an elephant attack on a hunting trip. I came here to look after the grandchildren. My daughter-in-law has no fixed income to repair the house. We were miserable and poor back then, and we are now as well. I sometimes think, was it worth what we did—clearing the forest for *chena* cultivation? The fact is, apart from day-to-day survival, we did not gain anything by *chena* cultivation. The only thing we have done is make the elephants hungry. Previously, at least they had plenty of food in the forest, though we did not.'

Pointing off into the distance, Rala continued talking. 'About two kilometres that way in the middle of the forest, there was once a water spring and a pond—the only waterhole in the area. Now, of course, people have built houses there and there is no more spring or pond. That was the spring where animals came to drink water during the dry season, especially elephants. When we came to the forest to hunt, we would stay close to the spring, hiding behind bushes to shoot a deer. Every time we came here, we had plenty of game to take home.

'But now, there are no more springs and waterholes. The streams have dried up, the forest is gone, the wildlife has disappeared, and the elephants are raiding home gardens in search of food. This is what we have achieved—not any economic development, not any improvement in our lives,' said Rala, sighing deeply.

By this time, people across all sectors of the rural community understood the traditional way of farming would not provide enough income to survive, let alone allow for a comfortable life. Young people were pursuing education so they could seek employment in other sectors. More and more students were winning government scholarships to enter university.

After I graduated, many students passed the scholarship examinations and entered high school in the city. Throughout the 1970s and beyond, several young people from our village pursued higher education.

My sister Kumari went to university in 1980, and later, a few other students—such as Jamis *Mudalali*'s son Nimal, and Siri *Mama*'s two sons and daughter—also entered university.

Mr Cyril and Anula's son, Kumara, entered university in 1987 to pursue a degree in the science stream.

CHAPTER 6

The Damage

Time passed without many changes to people's lives—except that they were getting older.

By the 1990s, the first generation of settlers was no longer working, and some had already passed away. The second generation was entering middle age, and the third generation had become the new farmers.

The livelihood of the villagers remained the same, except for families with children working elsewhere.

Many houses had undergone extensions, while some had been demolished and rebuilt. Some families had divided their original land parcels so their children could build houses. Next door to our place, Samithin's two sons had married and built their houses on either side of the old house. Our old friend Siriya, being a single man, lived with one of Samithin's sons—his nephew—while the old house had been abandoned. Navé had demolished our old house and built a new one. His three children were now studying in Kurunegala, staying with our elder sisters, Sudu *Akka* and Punchi *Akka*.

Jamis *Mudalali*'s son, Nimal, graduated from the medical faculty and was working as a doctor in Kandy. Sometime later, he transferred to Anuradhapura Hospital.

One day at the boutique shop, still the popular gathering place for the old generation, Banda said, 'We have not seen Silpa for a while. I wonder why he stopped coming here.'

'He is not well,' Gunarath *Mama* replied. 'He came to see me with lots of complaints. He told me he was urinating frequently, so I advised him to go to Yakalla Hospital and get some Western medicine. There are many good Western treatments for diabetes available now—more so than our traditional methods.

'He is mostly staying at home these days because he has aches and pains and feels like vomiting all the time. I went to see him yesterday. He complained of lower back pain and loss of appetite, saying he could not sleep well because he had to get up frequently during the night to urinate. Because of the muscle cramps and tiredness, he does not even feel like walking in the garden. He has always been such an active person, despite his age, so it is hard for him.

'I suggested he go to the hospital and get blood and urine checks done—this may be something beyond diabetes.'

Silpa's family did take him to the hospital, and the doctor advised he be admitted until the test results came in. Two days later, tests confirmed that Silpa had kidney damage and required frequent dialysis. As he was unable to get the treatment at the local hospital, he was transferred to the district hospital in Anuradhapura.

Silpa's story spread quickly.

One day, Podiya mentioned that his brother was experiencing symptoms similar to Silpa's, despite being middle-aged. People urged him to take his brother to the hospital for a check-up. When he did, it was confirmed that his brother also had symptoms of kidney damage, even though he was non-diabetic.

By 1992, otherwise healthy adults who were non-diabetic were being diagnosed with kidney damage, raising concerns within the community, as well as among health officials and researchers. This was not just happening in Huruluwewa but throughout the region. Silpa and several other elderly people passed away. Others required constant medical care, including blood transfusions, and the costs were overwhelming.

People were eager to find out the cause of the illness and why so many in the district were suffering.

News reports covered the issue, and television channels broadcast stories about the rising number of chronic kidney disease cases in the North Central Province and other areas. A week later, the Sunday newspaper published a full article about the crisis.

At the boutique shop, Podiya read the article aloud so everyone could hear. The article stated that medical professionals suspected that heavy metals from fertilisers were the cause. It also alleged that some opportunistic politicians in power had approved the importation of cheap fertilisers without conducting quality checks—simply to receive commissions from importing companies. This was not just the work of one politician but also corrupt government ministry officials.

'It's a crime,' the newspaper article said.

81

'This is exactly what Gunarath *Mama* warned us about thirty years ago—these pesticides and fertilisers are killing us slowly,' said Siri *Mama*.

It appeared that more and more poor-quality fertilisers had been imported and supplied to farmers at low costs, allowing corrupt officials to pocket commissions. The intention had never been to improve agricultural productivity or human and environmental health; it had always been about getting rich.

'Politicians benefited on two sides: subsidising fertiliser meant votes, and in addition, they received commissions from import companies,' said Podiya, angrily.

'Yes, while we suffer from all sides,' Banda replied. 'Subsidies meant the government had to spend massive amounts on farmer relief to "buy votes", and now they're spending even more to fix the health system.

'It would have been much better if they had provided good-quality fertilisers at market value, without any subsidies,' Banda reiterated.

According to the newspaper report, chronic kidney disease in North Central Province had become one of Sri Lanka's major health crises, affecting nearly 10% of people aged 15 to 70. The report stated that heavy metal contamination—previously absent from the environment—was now found in drinking water, fish, and root vegetables. The newspaper suggested that improper fertiliser application practices in paddy farming could be a major contributing factor.

Without any background knowledge of how much fertiliser to apply—and with subsidised fertiliser being so cheap—farmers had overused it. Though some government initiatives aimed to monitor the distribution of subsidised fertilisers, enforcement had been lax.

This was now a serious health crisis in rural communities, where most people depended on paddy and rain-fed farming for their livelihood.

People were advised not to drink water from their wells and instead to buy treated water.

Naturally, they were suspicious, thinking this might be yet another business scheme for someone to profit from.

'It's what Dr Piyal said years ago,' said Mr Cyril. 'Let alone finding food, now people have to buy drinking water.

Only a few people could afford to buy water, and the rest continued to drink well water, despite now being aware of the dangers. They had no choice.

Once the damage was done, a bold attempt was made to impose restrictions on chemical fertilisers and other agrochemical imports. This caused widespread concern among the farming community. Farmers were severely affected by the agrochemical shortage in the open market, which resulted in soaring prices. Unable to afford fertiliser, they soon found that the soil's natural fertility had diminished. Some farmers abandoned paddy cultivation altogether and blamed the abruptness of the restrictions, arguing that they should have been imposed gradually to allow people time to adjust to the new 'farming culture'.

As Gunarath *Mama* always emphasised, organic farming does not necessarily lead to a decline in agricultural production—

its trade-offs depend heavily on context. However, the sudden and total ban presented another challenge.

'The cheap fertiliser they gave to us now has become a curse on us,' old Herath *Mama* said.

People started to blame the government and senior officials for failing to check whether the fertiliser conformed to the required quality standards.

Mr Cyril shared his thoughts on the subject:

'The officials and so-called experts are in the pockets of the fertiliser importers. They're appointed as advisers to company boards, given vehicles, and paid a monthly stipend, so they won't say anything against them. In one of the panel discussions on TV, several experts claimed that heavy metals were naturally present in the soil and had simply leached into water sources. It was an attempt to protect the companies that paid them,' he said.

Gunarath *Mama*'s practice was to plough the paddy field before the rains and leave it fallow, allowing any remaining straw and plants to decay. Once the rains arrived, the decayed straw and plants became mulch, and bacterial activity transformed them into compost. The abundant rice straw, which was once considered waste, could be used as an ingredient in organic fertiliser or compost. Traditionally, poor farmers used it for thatching their roofs, but as that practice declined, the straw became available for spreading across paddy fields or burning, aiding in the recycling of nutrients.

Many people adopted this practice and achieved some success. They realised that although yields were lower, their total costs were significantly reduced.

You give something up, and you gain something else.

Thus, reliance on agrochemicals and fertilisers began to wane.

At one of the boutique gatherings, Siri *Mama* remarked that people always learned their lessons after the damage was done. 'Yet it still isn't too late,' he said.

Many villagers questioned why the so-called experts had not warned them earlier, before irreversible damage had been done to the natural environment and biodiversity.

A number of social issues also arose—particularly for families like Pédia's, who had been severely affected by kidney disease. As the main breadwinner, Pédia could no longer work and required constant medical attention, including costly blood transfusions at the district hospital.

His loyal wife, Emelia, did her best to sustain their livelihood. Their five daughters were growing up and needed financial support for their education, but at least they were dedicated students who performed well in school.

With Pédia's income completely gone, Emelia struggled to make ends meet. Some women suggested that she go to the Middle East for work, as many others had done, but she categorically rejected the idea.

'I will never leave Pédia and the girls alone,' she said. 'They need me now more than ever.'

Everyone knew she loved her husband and daughters more than her own life.

'Such a beautiful woman,' many said of her.

Emelia would wake up early in the morning and prepare a cup of tea for Pédia and herself, then start the day's work. She arranged with the boutique shop to supply hoppers in the morning and other short eats throughout the day. First, she cooked hoppers with batter prepared the night before, followed by coconut roti (flatbread with grated coconut) and coconut relish, known as *Pol Sambal*. She then prepared the younger children to go to school. On her way, Emelia took the hoppers and roti to the boutique shop. On some days, she also received orders for string hoppers and prepared them in advance with the help of eldest daughter, Emelin.

In addition to this, Emelia had plenty of work in the home garden. Pédia had planted an acre of *Nai Miris*—a small, very hot variety of chilli that fetched a high market price year-round. She had also started growing vegetables, which she sent to the Sunday market, along with the mushrooms they cultivated.

To support their mushroom business, Pédia had built a Cadjan-thatched wooden hut with timber racks for growing mushrooms. Now, Emelia tended to them. On some occasions, she also did laborious work in nearby houses—cleaning gardens, threshing, pounding rice, and grinding millet. She had taken up traditional crafts such as weaving coconut leaves for roof thatching and making mats and baskets from reeds and coconut leaves.

Emelia was incredibly busy throughout the day and had no time to rest. Seeing this, both Pédia and Emelin urged her to stop working as a labourer, as the work was too strenuous.

One day, Emelin said, 'Mother, I'm not going to school again, leaving you working from early morning to nightfall. I'm going to stay home to help you and look after our father.'

By this time, Pédia's back pain had worsened, and he could no longer walk without a stick.

'Don't talk nonsense!' Emelia scolded her daughter. 'If your father heard this, what do you think would happen? His life is his family; his dream is to give the best of everything to his children, and that means a good education. I don't want to hear this kind of talk again.'

'No, Mother,' Emelin insisted. 'I have thought about this a thousand times, and this is my decision. I am not a child anymore. I can help you with all the work you do. That way, we can earn more money to help Father, and we can educate my younger sisters. Do not say NO to my decision. I've passed year 8 in school and that is enough for me. My happiness, like yours, is to see my younger sisters continue their studies and do well in their lives, and to look after you and Father.'

When Podiya heard this, he tried to convince his niece to continue her schooling, saying he was always available if they needed him. Ever since Pédia became sick, Podiya would bring a portion of the paddy harvest to Pédia and provide whatever support the family needed.

Emelin's schoolteacher came to Pédia's home in the evening and tried to convince her to return to school.

'She has a brilliant future,' said the teacher to Emelia. 'She is one of the most gifted children in the school—our best student. She can speak English fluently and read and understand any book.'

Emelin respectfully told the teacher she did not want to see her parents suffering; she wanted to help.

'My four younger sisters will fill my gap,' she said. 'I want to give them a brilliant future.'

Despite Pédia and Emelia's repeated request, Emelin stayed home to help her mother and take care of her father.

'What this fertiliser has done to us!' Pédia would protest. 'We drank the polluted water, and we are still doing that! There is no other way to find water except to drink our own well water – we can't afford to *buy* water!'

Once a week, Emelia took Pédia to the hospital for dialysis. Emelin was not allowed to go, in case they missed the last bus and had to spend the night at the bus stand. It was never easy; they had to catch the 6 AM bus to Anuradhapura, but the bus service was erratic. Some days, it was an hour late, and by the time they reached the hospital, it was too late to get the dialysis done that day.

The hospital in Anuradhapura was the only one in the district with a dialysis centre, so patients came from all over for treatment. Some serious cases required dialysis two or three times a week.

On dialysis days, Emelia packed rice and curry for lunch and took a water bottle with her in a carrying bag. While waiting at the hospital, they often had the chance to talk with other patients from distant villages. Some days, they saw children—10- to 20-year-olds—needing dialysis. It broke Emelia's heart.

'These children's lives are ruined by this disease,' she said. 'This is what the "gift" of subsidised fertilisers given to poor farmers has created.'

As the hospital visit took almost all day, Podiya told Emelia he would get his brother to take him to the hospital and Emelia could stay home. He was very sad to see his wife and daughter tirelessly working. He regarded it his duty to provide them with a comfortable life, and now the unexpected had happened and he could not do that. When the unexpected happened and things could not be explained, the villagers would say it was because of karma, and this was Pédia's thinking, too.

One day, he was sitting on a wooden stool under the guava tree in front of the house, remembering his younger days when he and Emelia had met and become married. Emelia was his uncle's daughter and lived in his ancestral village in Kurunegala.

Both of them had attended school only up to Year 5 before staying home to help their parents with housework and gardening. This was typical for poor families at that time. Even if a student was bright, they simply could not afford to continue their education.

During one of his visits to his ancestral village, Pédia had asked Emelia if she would marry him and move to Huruluwewa. He was a handsome young man, and Emelia, a well-mannered, beautiful young woman.

Emelia had been waiting for him to ask, and now the day had come.

'I'd be happy to live in Huruluwewa,' she told him, willing to leave behind her parents, siblings, and village.

They went to Emelia's parents together and expressed their intention to marry. Upon returning to Huruluwewa, Pédia told his parents, and both families were pleased. Three months later, in a simple wedding attended by close relatives and friends, Pédia and Emelia were married.

Emelia had some idea of the difficulties she might face in Huruluwewa, but Pédia had explained further:

'The dry season is harsh in every way; sometimes, we don't even have water nearby to bathe. But the rainy season is beautiful, and there's plenty of work in the fields and gardens.'

'But you said I don't have to work. Why?' Emelia had asked.

'Because I'm strong enough to take care of my family, and I will make you happy there,' he had promised her. 'We must give our children the best opportunities to succeed in school, unlike us, who had to stop after Grade 5. I want them to get a good education and have the best of everything.'

But now...

Pédia's tears flowed as he sat under the guava tree, thinking about Emelin's future.

CHAPTER 7

Siri *Mama*'s Story

Rural village life was generally simple and peaceful. The people had few wants, as most of them were paddy and *chena* cultivators. Typically, women had a great deal of power within the family, but the ultimate head of the family was the husband or the oldest male. It was common for fathers to pamper their small children while maintaining stricter control and discipline over their sons. This was also the case with Siri *Mama*'s family.

Siri *Mama* was a typical villager who observed the customs of the community and worked hard to provide a comfortable life for his family, ensuring his children received at least a basic village-level education. Being a close friend of Gunarath *Mama*, he also practised organic farming in his home garden but used a limited amount of fertiliser and agrochemicals in his paddy field. He rose early in the morning and went to sleep late in the evening. Throughout the day, he worked in his home garden to earn extra income.

Unlike many other farmers, Siri *Mama* didn't wait for rain to cultivate his paddy field, nor did he engage in *chena* cultivation.

He firmly believed, as Gunarath *Mama* did, that if land was properly utilised in the home garden, it could generate sufficient additional income without the need to destroy forests for *chena* cultivation. While most villagers grew chillies, eggplants, manioc, and pumpkins, Siri *Mama* started growing betel, a crop his father had cultivated in their ancestral land in the Kurunegala area. Since both men and women in the village had a habit of chewing betel, there was always a steady demand. He also planted areca nut trees along the edge of his land.

Siri *Mama* always said looking after a betel crop wasn't easy—it was just like looking after a little child, always needing care and attention. Betel vine was a perennial, evergreen climber. Siri *Mama* used manure, and the leaves of *Wetahira* (gliricidia) and *Keppetiya* (*Croton laccifer*) as fertiliser. In his plot, he grew four rows of betel vines and about twenty vines in one row. There were four plots to look after, involving constant care. All around the plots, he grew ginger, lemongrass, and turmeric as he believed they added extra flavour and a medicinal quality to his betel; whether it was true or not, no one ever questioned it.

Watering during the dry period was not easy, as he had to take water from the well and spray manually, and this had to be done in the morning and evening so the betel would grow healthy dark green leaves. If the plant became heat stressed, it would turn yellowish, and the betel would have very low value. During the harvest, at least once a week, he picked mature leaves from the bottom of the plants and packed them into dry banana leaves in a laden cane basket. He carried the basket on his head around the villages, as most of the local boutique shops sold his betel, and on some weekends, he took it to the Yakalla Sunday market.

On market days, he travelled with other villagers in a hired bullock cart, carrying vegetables and other produce. He didn't spend a single cent on personal comfort, bringing only the lunch and water his wife packed for him. His betel was always in high demand and often sold out quickly. Sometimes, boutique shop owners from neighbouring villages bought in bulk, allowing him time to browse through pop-up clothing stalls to buy items for his children. Almost every Sunday, when he returned home, he brought sweets for the children, who eagerly awaited his arrival.

Siri *Mama*'s eldest son, Aruna, was an exemplary young man. His conduct was admirable—whether in helping his parents at home and in the garden, excelling in his studies, participating in religious activities, or fostering friendships. He consistently ranked first in all his examinations.

His second child, a daughter named Aruni, was a lovely, innocent, and studious girl. As was common in Sri Lankan culture, Siri *Mama* affectionately called her 'My Mother'—a term of endearment for a beloved daughter.

The youngest son, Sirimath, was a cheeky but brilliant boy. Unlike his siblings, he often tried to avoid gardening.

Their adopted son, Simon, was also highly intelligent and dedicated. He took on many responsibilities in the home garden, particularly tending to the betel plots and ensuring they remained intact.

Siri *Mama* would go out with Aruna and Simon to the bushland to cut and bring home *Keppetiya* leaves for the betel plots. The boys also helped with composting, learning the layering technique: alternating soil with cow or chicken manure and leaves. Siri *Mama* kept a small flock of chickens, selling extra eggs to local shops. He also added neem leaves to the compost, explaining to his children how neem oil naturally repelled harmful insects without harming beneficial ones like earthworms, ladybugs, honeybees, and butterflies.

Through these lessons, the children gained invaluable local knowledge about sustainable village farming.

Like many villagers, Siri *Mama* and his wife, Menike, regularly visited the village temple, particularly on full moon days. Their children often accompanied them. Aruna, in particular, attended meditation sessions and became known for his dedication. Villagers admired him, as he dressed in a white national outfit and spent the entire day at the temple, just like an adult devotee.

As the children grew older, their maturity deepened. Aruna became increasingly involved in school debates, passionately discussing social issues such as 'Do we really need a religion?' and 'Caring for animals: When one species vanishes, does nature adjust itself?' He was always hungry for knowledge and a voracious reader.

After the paddy harvest, Siri *Mama* and Menike went to Anuradhapura town to buy new clothes for the children and jewellery for Aruni. Though she was still a small girl, Siri *Mama* wanted her to have her more than enough jewellery when she grew up to be a young woman. As was typical in their culture, a daughter held a special place in the family, and he took great pride in providing her with everything necessary for a comfortable life. Aruni was the jewel in his crown. Every father's dream was to host a beautiful wedding for his daughter, and Siri *Mama* shared this sentiment.

At least once every two years, the family visited their ancestral village in Kurunegala. Both Siri *Mama* and Menike had some lands, about one acre each in their village, which they had given to Menike's brother, Nandiya, to look after. Any income off the lands Menike's brother enjoyed. On several occasions, Siri *Mama* suggested selling the land, but Menike opposed it. After all, it was part of her brother's family's livelihood.

Whether there was paddy cultivation or not, Siri *Mama* maintained a steady income from selling betel, eggs, ginger, and turmeric. Several villagers attempted to grow betel, but most failed as they were unable to provide the necessary care. Some were successful on a small scale. Siri *Mama*'s crop diversification became popular among the villagers. At one point, the agricultural extension officer visited and suggested securing government support to mill dried turmeric into powder for sale. This way, other villagers could also cultivate turmeric and earn extra income. If successful, locally grown turmeric and ginger powder would be available, reducing dependence on imported condiments for cooking.

However, this initiative never materialised.

During the harvest season, Siri *Mama* also bought local eggplants at above-market rates to support other villagers. He cut them into thin, linear slices and dried them under a solar tent dryer mounted on a wooden frame. He then sold them at the Sunday market. His efforts attracted the attention of other villagers, who began following his method to earn extra income.

As the children grew, Menike began mistreating Simon, showing favoritism when buying clothes or serving food. Several times, Siri *Mama* noticed that whenever she served fish, meat, or even fried salted dried fish, she only gave portions to her biological children. Whenever possible, Siri *Mama* discreetly gave his portion to Simon when Menike wasn't looking. He did not want to argue with Menike, as she never accepted his suggestions nor admitted fault, but he knew this couldn't go on. One day, when the children were not around, he confronted her.

Menike's reply was prompt and angry.

'He is doing much better here. If he'd stayed with his grandmother, he would have died of hunger. That bitch abandoned her child. She should have taken the child with her.'

'But we agreed to adopt him, didn't we?' said Siri *Mama*. 'We must look after him like our own. More than that, he is your brother's son.'

'She manipulated my brother; otherwise, he would not have been involved with her.'

In Sri Lanka in those days, an illegitimate pregnancy was always considered the woman's fault, especially if she was poor or from a so-called low-caste background, while the man remained blameless.

Rumours suggested that Menike's youngest brother, Nandiya, had been secretly involved with a beautiful young woman named Megia, who came from a low-caste family. When she became pregnant, he abandoned her. A year after the child was born, Megia married her cousin and moved to his village, leaving her son with her mother—apparently at her husband's request.

When Simon was two years old, Siri *Mama* adopted him as his own because the elderly grandmother was unable to care for him or provide a comfortable life. Thus, Siri *Mama* now had four children.

Siri *Mama* knew that questioning Menike further would only make her angrier, so he dropped the topic. As time passed, the children grew up quickly. Aruna and Aruni passed the scholarship examination and went on to study in a city school in Kekirawa, while Sirimath and Simon attended the local village school.

Then, much to the disappointment of Sirimath and Siri *Mama*, Menike asked Simon to stop going to school after Year 8 and start helping more at home. Sirimath cried and said it was cruel, as he loved his younger brother. He pointed out that Simon was exceptionally bright in school, but his protests fell on deaf ears.

Eventually, Aruna went to the university and graduated in management, Aruni became a medical practitioner, and Sirimath graduated in economics. All three settled in Colombo.

Meanwhile, Simon took over the farming in Siri *Mama*'s paddy field and home garden. He also bought an abandoned *chena* and began cultivating ginger, turmeric, and betel. With the healthy income he generated, he built a large, beautiful house on his land.

Simon eventually married Pédia's eldest daughter, Emelin, despite their ten-year age gap.

As time passed, Siri *Mama*, Menike, and Simon began to notice a change in Aruna and Aruni. Whenever they visited, they would leave for Colombo the same day. It seemed that rural life, devoid of modern comforts, was no longer tolerable for them.

During one visit, Siri *Mama* asked Aruna why he was leaving and not staying with his parents even for one day.

Aruna's response was shockingly aggressive.

'Old man, do you remember when you hit me with a wooden spoon in the kitchen? Do you know how much I suffered since then; you fool?'

Siri *Mama* was stunned.

'No one has ever talked to me like this—in my life!' he responded. 'I respect others and so they respect me. I even don't remember the incident. In any case, disciplining children is a parent's job.

'But beyond that, Aruni told us when we were not at home and you were, you used to hit Sirimath and Simon, and you threatened Aruni so she wouldn't tell us. Had I known this before, I would have given you a big smack,' Siri *Mama* said.

After Aruna left, Siri *Mama* and Menike talked about it and expressed their concerns as to how a once exemplary boy had somehow been converted into a demon. From that day onwards, Aruna stopped coming to the village.

Whenever he came to the village, Sirimath stayed at least a few days with his parents, and sometimes he stayed with Simon at his new house. He went out to meet his childhood friends in the village. He was a down-to-earth person, many people said in appreciation.

Eventually, Aruna returned and told his parents he was getting married in three months' time to a girl he'd met in Colombo at his job as senior secretary in a ministry. Not many details were given about the girl.

'Three months is time enough for me to arrange and prepare all the local sweets and rice for the homecoming,' said Menike. 'We must invite all our relatives from the ancestral village and, of course, everyone here in this village.'

She turned to Siri *Mama* and told him he would need to arrange for the house to be painted and to find bananas for the wedding.

'You can do that with Simon,' she said. 'We have to treat all the people in the village as this is our first wedding.'

Aruna laughed at this. 'You don't have to do anything. The wedding and homecoming are in Colombo. Only the two of you can come. I will send a vehicle—that is, *if you want to come*,' he said, pointedly. 'You can stay with Sirimath at his house.'

'What a shame!' Menike remarked. 'It is a tradition—we invite our close relatives and the villagers. You are the eldest son, and it is the first wedding for our family. We have lots of close relatives back in our ancestral village in Kurunegala.

'We have to have the homecoming here in this house!' she continued. 'You are our pride, and many villagers expect this.'

'That is the tradition,' said Siri *Mama*.

'There's no point in talking about it,' Aruna said. 'I don't care about your relatives or villagers here anymore. I am no longer "a villager." I am living in Colombo, and I like the city life.'

With that he announced it was time for him to leave, and he promptly departed, leaving his disappointed parents in his wake.

After Aruna left, Siri *Mama* said to Menike: 'That was not really an invitation. He just implied he wished we wouldn't attend the wedding.'

'I got the same message,' said Menike, 'but we will go. It's our son—our once-lovely, talkative, well-disciplined son.'

A week before the wedding, Sirimath came and took his parents to Colombo. He showed them around the interesting places in the city including the zoological garden to show them *Hurulu Kumari*, the rescued she-elephant. He also took them out for dinner at various hotels and restaurants.

Sirimath had prepared a small plastic bucket filled with sand, for his parents to spit into after chewing betels at home. What a thoughtful child, his parents agreed.

When Sirimath went to work, Siri *Mama* and Menike had the chance to talk, sitting outside the house. It had been a long time since they'd not had work to occupy their time.

'Are you feeling lazy and sick not seeing the betel plots?' Menike laughed.

'Of course, we are not used to this type of life,' said Siri *Mama*. 'We need to do something, but there's nothing we can do here. Anyway, Simon will look after the house and the betel plots, even better than me.'

Menike reminded him of when the children were young. 'Can you remember when little Sirimath and Aruni would come to sleep with you and listen to your stories?'

'Yes, of course,' he said, 'as if it were last night. They'd grab my hands—usually Aruni on the right taking my right arm and Sirimath on the left. They wanted to own me half each. You know the funny thing is, when I ran out of bed-time stories, sometimes I'd make them up.

'I'd usually start with "Once upon a time ..." which little Sirimath did not like. He would get annoyed and tell me not to start with that – that all my stories started with "Once upon a time ..." – "Aren't there any other times?" he'd say.'

Menike laughed and said, 'Remember when Sirimath was little, he'd always play with aluminium pans and spoons in the kitchen, pretending he was cooking for us?'

'Of course, I remember,' said Siri *Mama*. 'We used to call him "chef" and now he is doing just that. Last night's goat's meat curry and fried water spinach was very tasty. Goat's meat curry is one of my favourites.'

That morning, Sirimath had cooked chicken for his parents' lunch before he went to the office.

'I'm looking forward to that butter chicken for lunch,' said Siri *Mama*.

Sirimath had prepared the meat the night before and marinated it overnight. He also told them there was Indian flatbread, Parata, in the fridge which was very good with butter chicken. He said it was his favourite combination, butter chicken and Parata.

'Little cheeky brat; now grown up to a fine young man,' he continued. 'But I cannot imagine how Aruna and Aruni have changed so much!'

'Me either,' said Menike, sighing deeply.

'I remember you and my little brother, Nandiva, staying overnight in the hospital grounds until I delivered the child,' said Menike. 'He was supposed to be here at 11 PM. But the boy had the cord wrapped around his neck and wasn't delivered until 1:45 PM the following day.'

'Yes, we were awake until dawn,' Siri *Mama* said. 'That was why I named him "Aruna"—meaning "dawn".'

'It was the first boy in your family,' said Menike, spitting into the sand-filled bucket. 'Everyone was very happy that they now had a male descendant to keep the family line. Particularly your mother—she was overjoyed.'

She had kept a photo of Aruna under her pillow until her death—so much love for him from his paternal grandmother.

'He was showered with love from everyone,' said Siri *Mama*. 'As a one-year-old, he used to ride on my back—like riding an elephant. What a lovely child he was, but now…

'Now he doesn't even feel the need to invite any of his relatives to the wedding—not that he even likes to see them anymore. We may be villagers, but we have our traditions and ties to the family,' he continued, and then took a deep breath, signifying how painful this was for him.

'Remember, when he was five years old, he came with you to the garden wearing a sarong and a vest with his little mamoty. "I am also a farmer," he announced and attempted to work,' laughed Menike. 'I kept his mamoty in the corner of the firewood shed. It's still there.'

'Of course, I do.' These were the only words Siri *Mama* could manage in response.

'That lovely child has changed so much now,' continued Menike. 'In those days, when he stood or sat down, he'd imitate you. He used to say we were lions, after hearing your stories on the history of the Sinhala people.'

With this, Menike stood and said, 'Let's go and have some lunch.'

'I am also hungry now, said Siri *Mama* as he walked into the house.

On the wedding day, Siri *Mama* and Menike met their daughter, Aruni, who had not come to see her parents for years. She was beautifully dressed and with a man. Sirimath told them he was the man who was going to marry Aruni.

Siri *Mama* and Menike were the only people there dressed in typical Sri Lankan national dress, and they sat in the corner of the hall. Almost all the guests were talking in English, so they could not understand what was being said. The bride looked beautiful and was brought to the hall by her father.

Siri *Mama* said to Menike, 'Soon I can give my daughter away in marriage. It's my dream.'

'It's the dream of any father,' Menike agreed.

Two years later, Aruni came home and informed her parents the wedding would take place in a church. But she did not invite them. Instead, she said, 'We don't want to have villagers in our wedding. It's in a Western-style church. We live in the city; we do not belong to the village anymore.'

Probably she had learned this from Aruna, thought her parents.

His eyes filled with tears, Siri *Mama* said, 'Don't do this to us, my daughter. I have been dreaming of this day. I have collected jewellery for you since you were a little child and hoped to see you wear it on your wedding day.'

'Uh-huh … who cares?' said Aruni. 'The jewellery is old-fashioned. I don't like it, and I won't wear it.

'You have insulted me,' she continued. 'Actually, not just me but all of womankind. Do you know how much I have suffered?'

'I never caused that,' said Siri *Mama* with tears flowing down his cheeks. 'I never hurt my daughter. I loved you and treated you like my mother; I even called you a pet name *Mage Amma* (My Mother).'

'You wore a ladies' sanitary towel as a mask,' said Aruni. 'You went to the boutique shop, and people laughed at you, insulting women. Boys teased me at school when I was small. Do you not understand how much embarrassment it has caused me?' said Aruni.

To this, Menike abruptly said, her eyes wide open and eyebrows raised, 'Oh, dear me, why do I have to listen to this?'

With an apologetic tone, Siri *Mama* tried to explain: 'I thought it was a new kind of mask, and I had not seen them before. Your mother did not wear them. We are poor farmers, my daughter. All my life, I have worked hard to give my children the best of everything. This is unbearable. It is our sweat and hard work that fed you and allowed you to become educated and get a good job. Children should not show their power to their parents when they are old. I have heard about these kinds of children but never seen them before. Now my own children have fallen into this category.

'In any case, I am sorry if it caused you any embarrassment,' he continued.

'You apologise properly to me for what you did,' Aruni replied, sharply.

'I just did,' said Siri *Mama*, firmly. 'Beyond that, if you cannot understand, it is your problem.'

She grabbed her belongings and handbag, took out her car keys, and left in a huff.

'Both Aruna and Aruni think they are perfect,' Menike said, watching her drive off.

That evening, Siri *Mama* went to see his friend Gunarath *Mama* to talk and get some relief from the incident.

'Aruna and Aruni were some of the best children we had ever seen, but I cannot believe how they have changed. They have been successful in their studies and got good jobs … it shows education does not always make an "educated" person,' said Gunarath *Mama*. 'What are you going to do with Aruni's jewellery then?'

'Menike told me she packed them into a bag and took them with her, perhaps to exchange at a Colombo jewellery shop,' Siri *Mama* replied.

'Uh … puh … don't worry, whatever patterns change with time, gold never changes. She will one day remember what this gold represents—your sweat … from your betels,' said Gunarath *Mama*.

'Some children do not recognise how much their parents sacrifice to give them a better life. When parents get old, some children neglect them just like a rotten fish,' said Siri *Mama*.

'You know, Siri,' said Gunarath *Mama*. 'Back in my village, my elder brother's children, like yours, were well-educated, and two of them now live in Australia and are not coming back here. Another three of them are working in the city. They convinced him to sell his lands and the house, promising they would take their parents to Colombo and look after them as they are old now. My brother and his wife had lots of lands, and they agreed and were happy. They thought at least they would have their children to look after them in their old age. They could spend time with their grandchildren. That is the ultimate happiness of any grandparents.

'You know what happened? After taking them to Colombo, those three monster children kept their parents one week each just to show them they were keeping their promise. After that, they took them to a home for elders somewhere in Horana. That was it—none of them visited, let alone looked after them. One year later, they died in the home for elders, and the children never even attended the funerals. We heard about it three months after their deaths.

'This is what happens with some children; they just dump their elderly parents as rubbish, after getting all the comforts and benefits. Elderly parents become a burden. They are born as humans but live like demons … not even animals would do this kind of thing.

'It's unfortunate, but now you have done your part, and you shouldn't worry,' said Gunarath *Mama,* comforting his friend.

As Siri *Mama* took his leave, Gunarath *Mama* mentioned he was going to the temple that afternoon with evening tea should Siri *Mama* want to join him, and they could talk with the monk.

In the late afternoon, both Siri *Mama* and Menike went to the temple with ginger tea and betel for the monk. Gunarath *Mama* was already there. After visiting the Buddha house, they went to the *Vihara*, where the monks lived. After paying their respects, both Siri *Mama* and Menike sat on the mat in front of the monk.

The monk said, 'Gunarath already told me you are worrying about your elder son and daughter not respecting and loving you. Everyone in this village knows that you raised them well, providing the most comfortable life possible for them and educating them. You have done your best, so you must be happy. Do not expect anything from them, not even a word of thanks or love. People change—nothing is permanent in this world. They may realise one day and come to talk to you out of respect.

'What you both need to understand is this—love and attachment are different. Attachment is what you are expecting now—their respect, and for them to visit you, and so on. That is for your own happiness. Love is different: if your children are happy, then you should be happy as well. Remember, attachment always leads to suffering; if you lose, as in this case, it is suffering. In the end, we must *let go of everything*, including ourselves, so it is not worth worrying. But love always keeps you happy; and therefore, cultivate love for your children, love for everybody.

'This is why our great religion teaches us suffering comes as two arrows. The first arrow is inevitable; we all suffer through birth, old age, sickness, and death. This will come in different forms. If someone abuses us, and if we get hurt, that is suffering. That is the first arrow. Even enlightened beings get the first arrow. No one can avoid it.

107

'But if we suffer every time when we think about it, then that is the second arrow. It all depends on how our mind has reacted to it or how we perceive it. Some people suffer their entire life, thinking of past incidents, over and over again. This second arrow is the most painful, and enlightened ones don't have it. If we let go of it, the second arrow will not hurt us.'

Two weeks later, Sirimath came home and said that he was not going to Aruni's wedding if his parents and Simon were not invited. He further said that he was still a villager, even though he lived in Colombo. This he had already conveyed to both Aruna and Aruni.

Both Siri *Mama* and Menike pleaded with him not to do that, as it would be embarrassing for his only sister. They asked him to say, if someone asked, his parents were not well, which was why they were not attending the wedding.

Later, Sirimath told them that Aruna had brought Aruni to the wedding hall of the church where the ceremony was held. He had done as they had asked and attended the wedding, even though he hadn't wanted to.

The following year, Sirimath went to Canada. Before his departure, he came home and met Simon and his school friends. He went to his old school to see his former teachers and to the temple with his parents to receive blessings from the monk.

Sirimath asked Simon if he would take care of their parents, and if he needed anything, to ask him so that he could contribute financially. He said he would come home at least every second year to see them.

As promised, Sirimath telephoned home at least once every month. A year later, he said he met an English-speaking girl, Sarah, and they were going to marry soon. She was an accountant and worked in a bank. After that, they intended to visit Sri Lanka. Six months later, he sent home photos of the wedding. Both Siri *Mama* and Menike took them to show Simon. It was a simple, yet beautiful, wedding. Some of Sirimath's friends living in Canada had attended, though not any family members. The bride was a beautiful girl.

As their visit home was approaching, Siri *Mama* asked Sirimath how he should prepare the house. Would she be able to bear the heat? What food would she like to eat?

Sirimath told him she was more of a villager than all of them and a down-to-earth girl and not to bother with anything.

They arrived at the end of Sirimath's second year in Canada, staying a week in Colombo where they caught up with Aruna and Aruni and their families and visited the beaches down south and Yala National Park.

From the day they arrived home, both Sirimath and Sarah lived like villagers. Sirimath had to do lots of tireless translation during conversation. He has already taught her a few important Sinhala words:

Ayubovan – Sinhala greeting: 'May you have a long life.'

Mata bada gini – 'I am hungry.'

Kohomada Ithin – 'How are you?'

Bohoma Isthuthi – 'Thank you very much.'

Since Sirimath enjoyed cooking, Sarah was already familiar with Sri Lankan spicy food and was keen to learn more from Menike. She particularly liked *Pol Sambal* (spicy coconut relish) and *Polos Embul* (spicy young jackfruit cooked with coconut milk). She even once tried salted dried fish, but she didn't like it as it was too salty and, of course, there was that 'strong pungent smell'.

As it was January, the paddy fields were already cultivated, and Sarah went with Menike and some of the other women to see the fields. She worked with Siri *Mama* and Menike on their betel plot and vegetable garden, almost like a typical village woman. She wore a half-saree with a jacket.

Sirimath had told her their family's story well before their marriage.

Sarah came from a wealthy family; her father's family owned a timber mill and agricultural land in Canada. Yet they were simple, humble people. Sirimath had told them this once before, and now Siri *Mama* and Menike could witness it firsthand.

When Sirimath and Sarah stayed at Simon's house, she learned how to make hoppers from Emelin in the traditional way, cooking over a wood fire so that when she went home, she could cook them for her parents, she said. Emelin managed to speak English slowly, though not perfectly, and Sarah could understand if she paid close attention. Within a few days, Sarah and Emelin became good friends.

Sarah told her she had heard about her sacrifice for the family when she had stopped going to school to help her mother after her father fell ill. 'That was a very admirable human quality,' Sarah said.

'Yes, it all ended in success,' said Emelin. 'All four of my sisters graduated from university and are now doing well. Unfortunately, my father couldn't see them graduate,' she said, her eyes filling with tears.

Sarah learned from Siri *Mama* how to make an organic toy crown with jackfruit leaves.

'One day, when I come here with children, I will make crowns for them,' she said. 'I can also make them with maple leaves in Canada.'

Sirimath told her his father had made them for him when he was little, crowning him and saying, 'You are my king.'

Two weeks later, Simon prepared his van, and they made a trip to some of Sri Lanka's historical and culturally important places, such as Anuradhapura, Sigiriya, and Polonnaruwa. Sarah thoroughly enjoyed her stay in the village and learned a lot about the country's rich history. She said the following year she would bring her parents to show them this beautiful country.

After a month's holiday, Sirimath and Sarah went back to Canada. Sarah said in two years' time, Siri *Mama*, Menike, and Simon's family should come to Canada for a holiday and she and Sirimath would show them the country. The villagers were talking about Sirimath and Sarah for months, and one day at the temple, the priest said that Sarah had showed them the way to live. She had been born and raised in a comfortable Western society yet lived in this village like a villager.

'After all, life is too short to be proud and arrogant,' he said. 'We are all one and our journey here is very short. Behaving in a proud, unpleasant way, showing little respect for others, is as bad as people who are always intoxicated,' said the priest.

Though no names had been used, Siri *Mama* and Menike understood he was talking about Aruna and Aruni.

On one occasion, Aruna had been invited to the village school's prize-giving ceremony as the chief guest. The school community, teachers, and parents respected him as a proud product of the school. Unfortunately, he refused to attend, saying he was too busy. Aruna and Aruni deliberately distanced from the village community and their poor relatives.

A month after Sirimath and Sarah left, Aruna and his wife, Sriya, came to the village with their one-year-old daughter. They stayed for three days, visiting Simon and a few of Aruna's school friends, who were village farmers. On hearing this, Aruni and her husband Anil also visited and stayed two days with Siri *Mama* and Menike. They told them they were immigrating to Australia and would come back after two years.

'Aruna and Aruni have now become humble,' said Menike, after they left.

'The foreign girl has shown them how to live and be humble,' said Siri *Mama*. 'The lesson she gave is not only for Aruna and Aruni, but for all those arrogant bigheads. As the priest said, we don't live here forever, and we can't take anything with us when our time comes to leave this world. The only footprints we leave behind here are our good habits. Those memories last forever.'

CHAPTER 8

Realisation

By mid-1995, all the first-generation settlers such as Gunarath *Mama* and Siri *Mama* had passed away, and the second generation were past middle age and getting older. The third generation was the most active in farming. Unlike their predecessors, they had received a good education, and some had worked overseas before returning. With the availability of electricity, almost every house was equipped with television and computers, so they were more connected with the rest of the world.

A notable third-generation young man was Kumara, Mr Cyril and Anula's son, who had graduated in science and was a resourceful person. From childhood, whenever his parents visited Huruluwewa, Kumara accompanied them to the village. During his university days, he visited the village several times with his friend Anura and took part in all activities, be it in the paddy fields, vegetable gardens, or village sports.

Gunarath *Mama*'s house was now occupied by one of his grandsons, a schoolteacher and environmentalist.

On his visits, Kumara often sought the views of the village's young people on issues such as deforestation, the impact of subsidised fertilisers, and the use of pesticides. The community expressed that the biggest problem they faced today was the same as the first settlers who had arrived in 1953, two generations ago. There were no marketing or transport facilities, nor was there any advice on selling their produce.

The problem was that after the rice harvest, people needed to sell at least a portion of the paddy to pay off their loans to the government through the cooperative society because they lacked storage facilities to hold on to their produce. As a result, private rice mill owners bought the rest of the paddy, often at prices they controlled. Farmers were compelled to sell, as this was their main source of income.

'Large-scale private rice mill owners have enough storage facilities to keep paddy for two or even three seasons,' pointed out Karuna, Herath *Mama*'s grandson, who had been a primary school friend of Kumara.

'The government does not want us to have storage and milling facilities because they are in the pockets of the businessmen,' he continued angrily. 'Unless we change this practice, the farming community will always be ripped off. The mill owners fund both political parties, so it doesn't matter who wins the election— ultimately, they, the businessmen, are the real winners. They control the market.

'Close to general elections, politicians sometimes come and distribute bags of rice to each family, claiming they are trying to eradicate the poverty in the rural community, but they vanish after the election. Then, five years later, they reappear to deceive the poor people again. These rice bags they distribute are not bought with their own money—it's the rice mill owners and other businessmen who provide them. And this is just a small part of what they rob from us!'

Karuna laughed derisively, then continued. 'It's ridiculous to distribute bags of rice to rice farmers. Instead, they should have built the infrastructure necessary for farmers to sell their produce at the right price, facilitated timely loans, and established storage facilities and markets for our goods.'

Karuna's friend Sunil spoke next. 'Politicians know it very well—when they give a small gift during an election, people forget everything they did or didn't do and vote for them again. It's the stupidity of the people.'

'But not anymore,' said Kumara. 'Everywhere we go, people say the same thing. But unless we change this practice, this country can never advance or develop. It's wrong to say that we are a third-world country. In fact, we are tenth-world country. The only way to change is to change the people first—the way they think. Otherwise, they will stick to their old habits and keep switching governments between the same two parties every five years. That's how it's been for the last 75 years. That is what we are doing now going around the country and explaining.'

Karuna reiterated that what they needed most were more storage facilities and marketing strategies so that farmers could directly reap the benefits of their work.

'It's true,' said Kumara. 'In fact, studies have shown that 30 to 40 percent of vegetable and fruit production goes to waste. The 20th century has passed with no significant improvements in agriculture, particularly in storage, marketing, and adopting new technologies. Successive governments came and went, making promises that were never realised.'

Karuna mentioned that he had worked in the Middle East for a time, in Oman, as a motor mechanic.

'It's common to see packeted dried vegetables—carrots, beets, sweet potatoes, eggplants, bitter gourd, and even jackfruit and mango—in supermarkets. Pickled onions, chillies, and cucumbers are also very popular there. Can you believe that Oman, a desert country, exports mushrooms and capsicum? If they can do that, why can't we? Where is the wisdom of our politicians and policymakers?'

Shaking his head in frustration, he continued, 'I have friends working in South Korea who tell the same story. At the moment, only a small number of people are doing it here in their "backyards," but it's not happening at an industry level. It's quite amazing what other countries are doing. For example, Thailand is exporting dried durian and making toffee with tamarind. These fruits are widely available here, yet there's no mechanism to develop any food industry making use of them. Our politicians and top bureaucrats only promote imports so that they can get a big commission from importers.'

Sunil added, 'Once a minister actually said, "There is no need to cultivate rice here, as we can import and distribute it to people at a cheaper price." That was their attitude.'

'During the season, when everyone planted *Kekiri* (cooking melon or cooking cucumber), you could see piles of it along the roadside. No one was interested. It's the same thing with eggplants, pumpkins, and tomatoes,' continued Kumara.

'All those losses of vegetables and fruits could be converted into a money-making industry. This is the only way to improve the economy of the people across the country. Our people are hardworking, but there is no mechanism to help them reap the benefits of their labour. Now that we have electricity and are developing solar panel technology, we can modernise our methods and even create employment opportunities for our youth.'

'We have been discussing this all around the country, and today's rural youth are quite knowledgeable. These views have become quite common. There is hope—a great hope—everywhere in the country,' said Kumara.

'Almost all the agrochemicals available to farmers have been contaminated with arsenic. According to reports, the highest amount was found in *Mada Pohora* (TSP). The import of millions of tonnes of TSP meant that thousands of kilograms of toxic substances—arsenic and other heavy metals—have been added to the environment, contaminating our land and water. The only way to reduce the risk is by encouraging farmers to minimise the use of imported chemical fertilisers and transition to organic fertilisers instead. But this should be a gradual transformation,' Kumara continued.

'For the last 2,600 years, farmers inhabiting the dry zone of Sri Lanka cultivated rice using irrigated water and organic fertilisers. There are no historical records of kidney damage until the early 1990s; now, kidney disease is on the rise in rural Sri Lanka, especially in the North Central Province.'

The discussion shifted towards pesticide use. Even though farmers were aware of the harmful effects of pesticides and the importance of protective gear, more than 50 per cent still did not use protective equipment when applying pesticides.

'People don't care,' said Sunil. 'I saw Podiya last week spraying pesticide without wearing a mask. I said, "Are you trying to get sick, Podiya?" You know what his reply was? "It's just for today.""

'But "just for today" will happen tomorrow too, and then the day after, and the day after that…'

'It's foolish,' Kumara interjected. 'Two of the most important things—one's health and the environment—are the least of people's concerns until things go wrong. People take them for granted, and it's a global issue.

'There is no mechanism at the village or national level to educate people on the correct use of pesticides. Scientific recommendations are ignored. There is malpractice in pesticide use—overuse, underuse, improper mixing, and application—and it's happening everywhere. Most of the problems at the user level stem from farmers' attitudes.

'We know that before the introduction of conventional chemical pesticides, paddy farmers used a wide range of traditional pest control methods.'

Kumara went on to mention that he had not seen any fish or tadpoles in the paddy fields or waterholes, nor had he heard the croaking of frogs or the howling of foxes.

'These now seem like fables or mythical stories to our generation; we've only heard about them from our grandparents or read about them in books,' he said.

It seemed that nearly all of the third generation strongly believed that agriculture had been a major source of environmental pollution, and they were now witnessing its harmful effects firsthand. There was also a widespread belief that protecting the environment was essential.

CHAPTER 9

The Promise

There had been a shift in people's thinking. This new generation was more concerned with human health, the environment, and agriculture, and they eager to work according to a management plan. While this shift had been happening for the last ten years, it had peaked in 2022.

Everyone was hoping for a new government with fresh agricultural policies.

Anura and Kumara were the leading figures travelling across the country, conducting meetings and educating people. Many attended these gatherings, where Anura clearly explained the general policies of the government they intended to form after the 2024 election. Anura was now a member of parliament and had assembled a strong team.

The village community organised a meeting and invited Anura. Mr Cyril and Anula arrived in the village a month before the event. However, Kumara had no time to come earlier and spend time with them.

The meeting date was announced, and the venue was set at the community playground adjacent to the temple reserve.

Anura was the country's beacon of hope. His simplicity, renowned honesty, charismatic attitude, and friendly nature attracted large crowds.

News of Anura and Kumara's visit spread to the local MP, who sent a messenger requesting to chair the meeting.

The organisers chased the messenger away, with Podiya saying, 'Tell your boss that his generation of politicians is finished. They've done nothing for rural farmers for the last 75 years—how are they going to change now with their empty promises? Go back and tell him that!'

Navé was instrumental in organising the event, along with Mr Cyril and Karuna, who served as the honorary secretary of the local branch.

People from distant villages arrived in hired tractors and trailers, lorries, and a few buses. The playground and surrounding areas were packed with people.

Kumara arrived with Anura two days before the meeting and stayed with his cousin and parents. Close friends of Mr Cyril and Kumara, along with Kumara's former teachers and schoolmates, gathered to see them.

After a brief introduction by the organisers, Kumara opened the meeting. He introduced himself saying, 'I need no introduction as I am from this village. My grandfather was Gunarathhamy, popularly known here as Gunarath *Mama*. I grew up with the farming community and many of you know me from my early childhood.

121

'At a very young age, I became very familiar with organic farming. I have worked in the paddy fields and helped my grandfather in his home garden. Many of the farming techniques and problems facing our poor farmers I learned by living and working with them, not by reading treasury and central bank reports. This was the main setback with leaders of the past seventy-five years—they came from elite families. For the first time in history, a common man, our leader, Anura, will lead the government and we will make the country once again "the granary of the east" as my grandfather used to call it.'

Kumara then introduced Anura to the meeting.

'Anura is my university friend, and his village is in Kalawewa area. He also hails from a farming family like us. He has been to our village and stayed in our house many times, and he has visited the paddy fields and areas of *chena* cultivation. He is not a stranger to our village.'

Thereafter, Anura addressed the meeting, and explained the broad policies of the agricultural sector they planned to adopt.

'The agricultural sector is the cornerstone in Sri Lanka's economy, with more than 70 percent of the population living in rural areas depending on agriculture for their livelihoods,' he said. 'Currently, this sector contributes to about 18 percent of the GDP and 30 percent of the employment. The agricultural productivity has declined in the recent past, particularly for rice, with only 60 percent of paddy field being cultivated.'

He looked out amongst the sea of people and asked, 'Why is this, do you think? What are the reasons?'

He went on to answer his own question.

'In all previous governments, there were no firm policies regarding the development of the agricultural sector. This explains why, at least in part, this population suffers from poverty. A large majority of the poor in this country live in rural areas.

'Since we gained independence, no government has developed or adopted the abundance of new technologies that has been developed in the world. When the British left the country, we had a strong economy without any foreign debts, second only to Japan in Asia. Today, we are second from the bottom, why?

'All our past governments did was sell state assets to survive their term. Isn't that true? In reality, we never had the 20th century.

'Our agricultural experts have analysed the reasons for the low productivity of the sector, which contributes only a quarter of a farming family's income. That is why farmers who cultivate paddy fields need extra income from *chena* cultivation—until we lost our forests.

'There has been no encouragement to grow alternative crops during drought years, no push for crop rotation, and no support for organic fertilisers. We encourage you to cultivate three seasons in the paddy fields, with the mid-season for mung bean or cowpea. If water is limited for paddy cultivation, these crops can still be grown in the same fields. This method naturally fertilises the soil, as these crops fix nitrogen. By doing so, we can utilise farmland effectively while minimising the use of chemical fertilisers.

'Did you know that the atmosphere is one of the largest fertiliser reserves, but we fail to use it? Crops like mung bean and cowpea can absorb airborne nitrogen and enrich the soil.

'We are not going to dump cheap fertilisers or pesticides onto our lands anymore.

'We have several plans to increase the income and living standards of farming communities. Currently, we have twenty experts working on our agricultural policy. Our goals include increasing domestic agricultural production to ensure national food and nutrition security, improving agricultural productivity for sustainable growth, and maximising benefits while minimising adverse effects. We will expand our agricultural exports and adopt more productive farming systems.

'We will also encourage environmentally friendly and health-conscious farming technologies, promote agro-based industries, and create more employment opportunities.

'You know what? One of our key advisers is Kumara's uncle, Dr Piyal. Many of you know him as an internationally recognised expert and retired university professor.

'Under our government, unlike in the past, no single person will have total control over decision-making in the Ministry of Agriculture. Instead, decisions will be made by a council of experts from various related fields—including seeds, soils, water management, agrochemicals and fertilisers, plant nutrition, storage and handling, economics, and marketing.

'Of course, there will still be a minister representing parliament, but I want to stress that the council will be responsible for decision-making, not a single politician, as has been the case for the past seventy-five years.

'One of our main focuses will be the impact of climate change. Until now, no serious work has been done in this area in Sri Lanka, despite significant global advancements.

'This is our vision for the agricultural sector. Together, we can achieve it.'

There was murmuring amongst the crowd, and many heads nodded in agreement as Anura continued his speech.

'The agricultural sector has not created secondary employment opportunities, as it has not been developed to absorb rural unemployment like other industries. Yet, dried vegetables and fruits have a strong global market. More than ever, dried moringa leaf powder is in growing demand.

'You all know that moringa can grow anywhere in the country. This could provide a major employment opportunity.

'Look at that fence over there,' Anura said, pointing to the fence line of the playground.

'I can see three moringa trees from here. Many of you plant moringa along your fences to harvest the bean pods, or "drumsticks." This tree lives for thirty to forty years and requires no fertiliser, little water, no pesticides, and no large plantation area. It can be grown along fences or in home gardens—and that is enough. If every household in a village like this grew moringa, it would be enough to support a small factory to produce moringa leaf powder.

'By promoting simple agricultural systems like this, we can bring employment opportunities to rural areas and, more importantly, generate much-needed export income.

'Many of you have witnessed firsthand the suffering of those in your village who have fallen victim to kidney disease. I was saddened to hear that Dr Nimal also passed away from kidney failure. Research has confirmed that the overuse of fertilisers containing heavy metals is the root cause of this illness.

'When the government suddenly stopped providing fertiliser subsidies, the agricultural industry collapsed entirely.'

'I heard this was foreseen by Kumara's grandfather, Gunarath *Mama*, many years ago.

'We will promote the production and utilisation of organic and bio-fertilisers and gradually reduce the use of chemical fertilisers. So, too, the use of pesticides and weedicides. Initially, we will ensure the timely availability of sufficient chemical fertilisers while promoting the production and use of environmentally friendly bio-pesticides through public and private sector participation.

'We will strictly adhere to plant protection regulations to prevent alien weeds, insect pests, and diseases from entering the country … and there will be strict implementation of testing and inspection regulations when importing chemicals related to pesticides.

'This is our vision,' said Anura.

Some people were still sceptical, suspecting that Anura was just another politician out to deceive them, as was evident in the way they asked questions.

'Why should we believe you?' asked one man. 'For the past seventy-five years, politicians have come and promised all sorts of things but never delivered. Is this going to be just another broken promise?'

'You have to give us the opportunity first, and then see the results,' Anura said, going on to emphasise the excellent team they had put together to govern, maintain law and order, eradicate corruption, and preserve human health and the environment.

'But first,' he added, 'you must believe us.'

CHAPTER 10

The Hope

After the meeting, Anura stayed for further discussions with the community. Many youths attended, including local students from universities and technical colleges. The gathering, held in an open space in front of the small community hall, was informal—more of a question-and-answer session than a speech.

Despite being in his late 70s, Dr Piyal had arrived the day before and stayed with Mr Cyril and Anula, who were very proud of their son's growing influence in the country alongside Anura. From the second generation, Navé came with a few others, but neither Siriya nor Samithin could make it as they were almost bedridden.

One of the young men opened the discussion.

'Almost everyone in our generation sees sustainable living as the way forward, and many of us have either studied or at least heard about "permaculture". However, most farmers are unfamiliar with this concept, and there's a lack of knowledge on how to proceed. Don't you think we need to launch a broad educational program?'

Dr Piyal stood up and cleared his throat.

'Certainly. Educating the community is the best way to introduce any new program. This was precisely what was missing in the past when it came to fertilisers and pesticides—until people started dying from kidney failure.

'That said, even if we introduced an educational program, how many people would actually attend? One of the biggest challenges is people's negative attitudes.'

'If you offer a free lunch or alcohol, they will all show up,' someone in the crowd called out. 'That's what some political parties do to attract people to their meetings—give them a lunch packet and half a bottle of arrack.'

Laughter rippled through the audience before Dr Piyal continued speaking.

'I totally agree that we need widespread educational efforts to popularise permaculture. But there's nothing new about it. Kumara's grandfather, Gunarath *Mama,* and people like Siri *Mama* practised it in this very area. They never used the word "permaculture", but what they did was exactly that.

'Permaculture is simply developing the agricultural ecosystem in a self-sufficient way. It's a type of farming system based on crop diversity, resilience, natural productivity, and sustainability. People would need to shift their mindset first for them to adopt this approach,' he continued.

'But let me give you an example. With the increase in tillage, different rotational fallow systems can increase paddy yield by promoting soil nutrient uptake and increasing the relative abundance of bacteria in paddy fields. If you asked your father or grandfather, they would tell you how Gunarath *Mama* added straw to the soil and kept it fallow for a period; the remaining straw he would burn to add ash to the soil, which was his potassium supply. In his garden, he arranged one type of plant to supply nutrients to others. He didn't use fertilisers or pesticides at all, but his harvest was second to none.

'In summary, it is basically a way of living self-sufficiently and sustainably by working with nature to grow your crops. Gunarath *Mama* was inspired by the natural forest—the way it derives fertilisers through decaying animals, leaves, and wood. In fact, every time he spoke about his method of farming, Gunarath *Mama* gave the natural forest as his example.

'This is what Anura and Kumara are explaining as they go around the country, meeting farming communities. It is absolutely not difficult,' said Dr Piyal. 'The solution is obvious, though it is not widely practised yet. As I said earlier Gunarath *Mama* practised it, and I heard that Simon and a few others are doing so now.

'We can visit tomorrow, if you would like to see his garden as he is still maintaining the practice adopted by Siri *Mama* and Gunarath *Mama*.

'The linkage between the paddy fields and the associated environment plays an important role in biodiversity. This is why, years ago, Navé's father told everyone to have bushes and trees around the paddy fields. He didn't have any formal education on permaculture or ecosystems, but he had knowledge gained over several generations.

'I have visited Cambodia, Vietnam, and Thailand several times during my overseas work. Rural communities there are like here in our own country, and they used to use pesticides and herbicides, mostly for vegetable farming. They have also introduced improved rice varieties, but they are very careful in applying fertilisers and pesticides.

'Why do you think that is?' Dr Piyal questioned.

The audience fell silent.

'In these countries, one of the most serious pests affecting rice seedlings is the golden apple snail. Interestingly, this snail is also a protein-rich delicacy and an important part of the local diet. Many farmers keep freshwater fish and crabs in their irrigation bays, and some even have small ponds in their paddy fields to raise them year-round.

'Because of this, they are incredibly careful when spraying pesticides or using chemical fertilisers. If you walk through a street market in these countries, you'll see many stalls selling live freshwater fish, including Lula fish (Snakehead Murrel), which they particularly enjoy—just as we do here.'

Dr Piyal paused for a moment, and a villager took the opportunity to ask a question.

'Without killing them, how do they get rid of the snails? If you allow them stay in the paddy field, won't they just eat the rice plants?'

'They pick them by hand from the rice bays,' said Dr Piyal. 'First, they drain the bays and then collect the snails. They keep them in small tanks or fishponds with other fish. Vegetables and even fish food pellets are good nourishment for the snails.

131

'We have discussed this at length. We know that the main problem with pesticides is that farmers often misuse them, either applying them too early or using excessive amounts. This destroys the natural enemies of pests, and some pests evolve and develop resistance, requiring even stronger pesticides over time.

'You know what? In Japan, the average size of a paddy field is smaller than yours. Here, you have three acres, but their average size is about one and a half acres. Yet, small-scale organic farms in Japan harvest 20 percent more than large-scale rice farms.'

'What is the secret?' asked Karuna.

'There is absolutely no secret,' said Dr Piyal. 'They get water for the rice field from upstream forest catchments, containing lots of leaf litter and organic materials with microbiological activity. This sustains the paddy fields, eliminating the need for chemical fertilisers.

'In Japan, only pesticides with the lowest levels of fish toxicity are used. Rice fields are carefully managed so that fish habitats remain undisturbed. Also, rice is grown and harvested only once or twice in the same paddy field. The chemical composition of waterlogged soil encourages the growth of microorganisms that fix airborne nitrogen. This constant nitrogen supply is accounted for when applying fertilisers.'

'So, by microorganisms, do you mean soil bacteria are essential in managing crops?' asked a young man from a neighbouring village.

'Of course,' said Dr Piyal. 'And the chemical composition can also be managed through crop rotation. After one season of paddy, if you cultivate a leguminous crop like cowpea, it will fix the nitrogen in the air.'

'Do you mean a cowpea plant can get nitrogen from the air?' asked Sunil.

'My answer is both "yes" and "no". No, because not directly,' explained Dr Piyal. 'But yes, with the help of bacteria named Rhizobium. These special bacteria stimulate the growth of nodules on the roots of leguminous plants. The bacteria help the plant by extracting nitrogen from the air, while the plant helps the bacteria grow by supplying carbon. It's a perfect relationship.

'If you dig a root of a cowpea plant, you can see these nodules. This is a prime example of how important it is to maintain the natural ecosystem and environment. It provides an invaluable service. We are all interdependent—we cannot survive without other living organisms.'

'And it is not just a kind of "subsidised nitrogen"—it is completely free nitrogen,' said Sunil, with a loud laugh, which caused several of the attendees to burst out laughing also.

Dr Piyal waited for the laughter to subside before continuing to speak.

'In Japan, the control of weeds is also interesting. Once the seedling has emerged in flooded rice bays, some farmers bring their ducklings in and they eat the weeds and the insects that feed on young rice plants. This complex multi-species system means no other external pesticides or weedicides are needed.

'It is now well known all over the world that the use of agrochemicals causes deterioration of wetlands. Biodiversity loss by pesticides and herbicides and the pollution of groundwater is immeasurable.'

'Excuse me, Dr Piyal, with all respect to you, I have a question to ask,' said Karuna. 'Are you saying the loss of biodiversity is happening elsewhere as well?'

'Yes,' Dr Piyal responded. 'Biodiversity in many tropical regions is under serious threat due to agricultural expansion and intensification. That's why the future of local ecosystem conservation depends not only on traditional protected areas but also on well-managed agricultural landscapes.

'We need a well-structured agricultural system—not just to produce food for humans but also to preserve the balance of our ecosystems.

'We must look at the paddy fields in different ways,' he continued. 'Beyond providing rice and other foods such as fish and freshwater crabs, paddy fields also deliver other ecosystem services such as regulating water quantity and quality, ground water recharging, flood control, decomposition of organic wastes, soil formation, biological nitrogen fixation, soil erosion and landslide prevention, and biodiversity conservation. The pest control services provided by natural enemies are important for maintaining crop productivity in environmentally friendly agriculture with reduced use of pesticides.

'I do not mean to lecture here,' Dr Piyal emphasised, 'but I must say this—organic farming is generally considered to increase the abundance of natural enemies and to enhance ecosystem services. These farming communities therefore need to be supported well to ensure their continued production and much-needed environmental services. However, poor management of agrochemicals, especially excessive application of fertilisers and pesticides, has caused problems such as the deterioration of rice quality, unstable yields, and environmental degradation.'

'So, there is far more for the government to do in terms of improving agriculture,' said Karuna. 'I mean—beyond just distributing subsidised fertiliser.'

The villagers were nodding their heads. They overwhelmingly agreed nothing had been done to improve agriculture on the government's part, and that all they were interested in was winning votes.

After a brief pause, Dr Piyal continued speaking.

'The overuse of chemical fertilisers can lead to soil acidification because of a decrease in organic matter in the soil. Nitrogen applied to fields in large amounts over time damages topsoil, resulting in reduced crop yields. Too much fertilising also causes plant stress and weakens them, making them susceptible to diseases and insect attacks, particularly sap- feeding insects.

'Countries like Vietnam have banned certain weedicides completely,' he continued, 'while here they are still in use.

'Now you know that farming is not just about preparing the land, putting seeds in the ground, and then applying chemical fertilisers and pesticides.

'In our country, we have been good at developing high yielding rice varieties; this has been good research. But nowadays, farmers need to know what type of soil they have, what kind of crops are most suitable for the land, how much and when to apply fertilisers, if necessary, what is the change in demand pattern, and so on.

'My experience in countries in Southeast Asia—Thailand, Cambodia, Laos, and Vietnam—with farmers and government officials helped to formulate how to apply fertilisers and manage pests in rice farms. Now, remember that Thailand is the world's second largest rice-exporting country and Vietnam is the third. Also, their staple food is rice—whether boiled rice or noodles— it's always rice-based. In those countries, each person consumes 125 to 150 kilograms of rice per year.

'That's a lot of rice. And it's the same here. But the amazing thing is they have excess and still export.

'So, there you have it—these are some of the changes that Anura and Kumara want to bring about,' said Dr Piyal. 'I highly commend them for what they are doing.'

Karuna commented that the fertiliser subsidy program was one of the longest lasting, most expensive, and most politically sensitive policies implemented to promote rice cultivation.

Many other attendees nodded in agreement, and one pointed out that most of the corruption had started after 1977, when the government allowed private sector companies to import.

'Cheap non-compliant fertilisers were imported and distributed—and the poor are paying the price. We don't even know how long this kidney disease will last,' he said.

'I read somewhere that environmentalists conducted research on how heavy metals, like cadmium, from fertilisers pollute waterways. Cadmium is linked to chronic renal failure. But no one has taken any action.'

'Do you know why no action was taken?' asked Dr Piyal.

Karuna answered, 'Obviously, because politicians and government officials feared losing their commissions from import companies.'

'That's true. But you see, Karuna, there is another reason—a political one,' said Dr Piyal. 'We all know that paddy cultivation provides livelihood opportunities for many rural communities in the country. This means whatever government you have elected has been under constant pressure to continue the fertiliser subsidy. Otherwise, it would damage the political power base of the ruling party, whichever it is.

'However, the fertiliser subsidy was eliminated between January 1990 and October 1994, then reintroduced in 1994, leading to fixed retail price levels. The subsidy was targeted only to small paddy farmers (owners or tenants) who control less than five acres of land, as many paddy farmers are smallholders, with less than five acres of land under their control.'

'You know what actually happened, Dr Piyal,' said Podiya. 'My brother was a tenant farmer the same as several others in the village. To get the subsidy, they had to provide documentary evidence proving legal ownership of land, which was impossible. So, the landowners got the subsidised fertilisers and sold it to the tenant farmers.'

'This is another type of corruption, though it is small scale,' laughed Sunil.

'This means corruption is at all levels, top to bottom,' said Karuna.

'That is very true,' said Dr Piyal.

After listening to the various opinions expressed in the meeting, Anura said, 'In those days, the fertiliser subsidy policy was coupled with a paddy procurement policy, which required farmers to supply a fixed portion of paddy to the government at a pre-specified price below the market price. Therefore, it was not really a subsidised price.'

'Our aim is to gradually reduce the use of synthetic fertilisers. It is true they make crops grow faster and bigger than organic fertiliser, such as animal manure. But the use of organic fertiliser has other benefits.'

'Agriculture is a complex challenge,' said Dr Piyal. 'It's the **leading driver** of deforestation, biodiversity loss, land use, freshwater withdrawals and water pollution, worldwide.

'The obvious solution, then, is to implement more policies focused on reducing environmental impact,' said Anura. 'But this assumes that all policies are effective and don't create trade-offs with food production or socioeconomic outcomes. Unfortunately, that's not always the case.

'We all witnessed what happened in mid-2021, when the government **abruptly banned** chemical fertiliser imports. This caused devastating losses in the country's food supply. Rice production plummeted by nearly 40 percent between 2021 and 2022. The production of key export crops, such as tea and rubber, also fell significantly. The country spiralled into an economic crisis.

'The lack of planning and foresight made this policy catastrophic. Farmers had no time to find alternative nutrients or learn how to optimise organic farming. This is a clear example that having a policy in place doesn't necessarily mean it will produce good outcomes.

'Effective policies must consider trade-offs and priorities, not just in terms of national outcomes but also the global environmental and socioeconomic impacts.

'This is our aim,' said Anura.

CHAPTER 11

Wisdom of the Old

In 2023, I joined my remaining siblings—Navé, Seela, and Kumari—and visited Huruluwewa. I had returned to Sri Lanka from Australia, where I now lived, for a holiday. After reminiscing about our childhood memories, we decided to visit the paddy field where we had worked as children.

Navé's son, Thilina, prepared his van, and his wife, Thushani, along with their two little daughters, Nethuli and Dinuthi, joined us. So did the grown-up child, Sethuni, with her mother, Asanka, and father, Aruna. Erranka and her husband, Chandana, along with our niece, Ranjani, had already left an hour earlier, preferring to walk and take in the sights of the paddy fields and surrounding areas along the way.

It had been 50 years since I had last set foot in this field.

Pointing to a rice bay, Navé said, 'That was where you and Siriya had a vegetable plot. Now, all that belongs to history.'

After walking around the field, we made our way to the far end, where the natural drainage channel had once been. The channel had deepened and widened, and there were no more bushes, hedges, birds' nests, or even reeds. Five years ago, Navé had planted some banana and jackfruit trees along the drainage channel. Along the channel reservation of some other fields, people had planted coconut trees—some of which had grown tall and were now bearing fruit. It was sad to think that officers had once asked our father to pull out the perennial trees that had stood here. By now, they might have realised their importance.

Seela and Kumari stood on the bund of the last bay.

'This was the spot where we used to pick *Mukunuwenna* (sessile joyweed), *Polpala* (knotgrass), and *Sarana* (watercress), but they are no longer here,' said Navé. He then pointed to a particular spot. 'And that's where you used to build a stick-dam across the drainage channel to store water, Senevi.'

I remembered it well—building a dam across the drainage channel with a spill and watching eagerly as the dam filled and spilled over—only to return the next day to find it breached and having to rebuild it all over again.

After walking through the field, we gathered at the rock, where Navé spoke with emotion.

'All my younger siblings know that when we came to this field fifty or sixty years ago, it was full of life. During the rainy season, when we ploughed the land, there were birds everywhere, croaking frogs, small fish, freshwater crabs, and so much more. I haven't heard a fox howl in more than fifty years. The younger generations wouldn't even recognise that sound.

'You don't hear any of nature's voices anymore. They've vanished—because of us.

'But we didn't know it was wrong at the time. Every solution we introduced only created a new problem. We didn't really solve anything—we just started a chain reaction of issues.

'Let alone the fishes, frogs, crabs, and birds—if you dig the soil, no earthworm can be found here either. This was the result of introducing agricultural chemicals without any plan.

'Gunarath *Mama* is gone, but he had wisdom. He saw this coming. He once said that chemical fertilisers would be the beginning of the end. He warned that a small increase in yield wasn't worth it if it meant destroying the life of the land. When the soil loses its natural fertility, we become completely dependent on artificial fertilisers. When there's no natural way to control insects, we become entirely reliant on pesticides. And those cost money. So, in the end, the increased yield is no real gain. That is what has happened now. Many people have abandoned their fields—some say as much as 60 per cent this year alone—because farming is no longer worth it.'

He took a deep breath before continuing.

'I still cultivate our field because it is part of our lives. I attended several meetings with Anura and Kumara when they came here. They explained their master plan for agricultural development. What I liked most was their idea of gradually reducing chemical use and increasing organic fertiliser, like Kumara's grandfather once did. If this plan takes shape, it will be like returning to the old wisdom, and biodiversity will return. It may take time, but it will happen.'

Turning towards Thilina, Navé finally said, 'I may not live to see that day, but you and your children will. Even though

Senevi has two sons and a daughter, they live in Australia. We have not seen them in years. The three of you are the last male descendants of our parents, and you are the only one living here. So, in front of my siblings, I have a request to make.'

A hush fell over the group. The men stood with their arms crossed and heads bowed, while the women listened with tears in their eyes.

'I last saw Senevi's three children when they were young— more than twenty years ago. I know they have grown up well, received a good education, and are now working in Australia. It is unlikely they will ever live here, but one day, they may visit. If they do, take care of them. Look after them. If possible, serve them a meal with rice from this very field.

'All of you—and even those who are not here—must understand that my parents and siblings shed their blood, sweat, and tears in this field. Tears, because when a crop failed, we "harvested only tears". We have walked every inch of this land. We are an inseparable part of the field.

'Anyone who eats rice from this field keeps a strong bond with the family.

'I am sure that one day, Senevi's children will come to see where their father grew up. If not them, then their children or grandchildren will. It is human nature to seek one's roots. We are all one—one and only one—though we grew up and now live in different places in the world.

'When that day comes, they will want to see this rock—the place where Senevi heard

143

the howl of the last fox.

He paused for a moment before making his final request.

'When I die, after my cremation, bring my ashes here to this rock.

'This is where our father used to sit during tea and lunch breaks while we worked in the fields.

'When you bring my ashes, sit here for a few minutes and scatter them around this rock.'

My heart swelled with love—love for my brother, for my family, and for this land that tied us together.

'The same for me,' I said softly. 'If I take my last breath here in Sri Lanka.'

Author's other published works

Order from: https://inspiringbookshop.com

1. Narayana Family – *Brief History and Demography* (with Kumari Narayana)

2. A Silent Pain

3. Silver Bangles and Gold Bangles

   with three other short stories
   -Be My Daughter
   -The Deeds
   -Navigating through Loneliness and Aloneness

www.ingramcontent.com/pod-product-compliance
Lightning Source LLC
Chambersburg PA
CBHW052115030426
42335CB00025B/2992